Twenty-Se Blues

A Memoir of World War II

Robert L. Thornton

Twenty-Seven-Eighty Blues
by Robert L. Thornton

Copyright © 1993-2007 Robert L. Thornton. All Rights Reserved.

First Printing: April 2006
Second Printing: December 2006
Third Printing: September 2007

ISBN 13: 978-1-933817-38-5

Published in the USA by
Profits Publishing of Sarasota, Florida
http://profitspublishing.com

Twenty-Seven-Eighty Blues

is dedicated to the memory of my good friend and
compatriot

THOMAS J. SHANAHAN

And to all the other brave men of the 92nd Bomb Group
who went down fighting and did not live to tell their
stories.

Let us hope their sacrifice was not in vain…
and that they are always remembered.

Author's Note

Sometime after World War II I was told that I was suffering from Post Traumatic Stress Disorder. Because I found it so difficult to talk about my experiences in that war, my analyst suggested that putting them down on paper might help. He was right. I found writing about them, although not a cure, was very therapeutic. I also see it now, as a legacy to my descendants.

Although true, a story like "Twenty-Seven-Eighty Blues" could never be told without the use of some poetic license ... for example: routes, conversations, and some chronological events other than missions.

I must say that my description of the missions are as I perceived them. Since we all sat in different places, I am sure there could be nine slightly different versions of the same mission.

The first version of "The Blues," no more than a bunch of notes, was compiled in 1946 while they were still fresh in my memory. Other versions followed as new revelations and recollections occurred. Therefore, as time goes by, new versions became longer and more accurate.

A whole new dimension opened up when I joined two organizations: The Eighth Air Force Historical Society, and the 92nd Bomb Group Memorial Corporation. I *was then able to communicate with many compatriots, and we were able to compare notes.*

A trip to the Imperial War Museum in Duxford, England in 2001, and attending the 92nd Bomb Group reunion in Savannah, Georgia, in 2002, prompted the writing of this version.

I would like to thank 92nd Bomb Group Archivist Bob Elliot, secretary/treasurer Irv Baum and pilot Al Vermeire, for their help in providing me with documents proving that I was on the Essen mission of March 8, 1945, and the Bremen mission on March 11, 1945. Because of some SNAFU, these missions are not shown on my service record.

I would also like to thank pilots Hank Lapinski, John Paul, Harry Culver, and artist Danny Darnell, for their valuable contributions.

Last, but not least, this project would never have been finished without the good advice and undying support of my good friends, Frank Zimmerman, sometimes known as Tim Fox, Judy Johnson, and John Blutenthal. A very special thanks to both of you.

Robert L. Thornton

Osprey, Florida
June 6, 2004

Foreword

Burr Ridge, Illinois,
Saturday, May 15, 1993

It was a beautiful Saturday morning and my birthday. After breakfast, over a second cup of coffee, I scanned the Chicago Tribune looking for something special to do today, and there it was. It said that the Confederate Air Force had a World War II B-17 on display at the Dupage County Airport.

This widely celebrated aircraft was once my Guardian Angel. It literally had taken me to hell and back many times. And now, after almost fifty years, I had to see her one last time. Also, it gave me an opportunity to share with my wife the aircraft that had once played such an important part in my life.

Arriving early we were first in line for a walk through the old war horse. My pulse quickened as I stood on the tarmac and saw her standing there in all her glory. She was a 1944 G, the last and best model ever made. But she looked much smaller today. I found it amusing that I was paying three dollars to board her. At one time, if you told me I would someday pay to do this, I would have said you were crazy. But now I felt that I owed her. I'm glad that someone is taking care of her and helping to preserve her memory.

Having paid the admission, we climbed a ladder and entered the nose hatch. In the old days there was no ladder, if... I went in the nose hatch, I would throw my chest pack chute in first, grab the top of the hatch like a chinning bar, and hoist myself in feet first. But in the old days I was only nineteen years old. On combat missions, the only men that went in by the nose hatch were the men up front, the navigator, bombardier, pilot, copilot and engineer.

Everyone in the back, the tail gunner, waist gunner, ball turret gunner and radio man, went in by the waist door.

Now this may sound crazy, but when I think of these guys today, I remember them the way they looked in 1944-45, and when I looked into the nose in 1993, in my mind's eye I could see bombardier, Ted Fossberg, checking out his bomb sight, and navigator, Bob Johnson, organizing his maps. Climbing up into the cockpit I saw pilot, Hank Lapinski, and, copilot, Whitey Holsinger, going through their preflight stuff, with engineer, George Jeager standing between them looking over their shoulders.

⌘

Going through the bomb bay I entered the radio room. My room. I sat once again in the radio operator's bucket seat and looked out the window on my left at the number one and two engines. Chills went up my spine. Every hair on my body tingled. I had once witnessed so many incredible things from that window.

From the radio room I entered the waist, and there I saw ball turret gunner, George Waldschmidt, with

Coming through the bomb bay door

At my desk in my own private room

his pencil like mustache, standing by the ball turret with a big grin on his face. Waist gunner, Les Brazier, was mounting a fifty-caliber machine gun in the left window, while tail gunner, Mal Abrams, watched. Then they vanished as we turned and went back to the real world through the waist door.

My head was flooding with memories and I was an emotional zombie as I caressed the smooth Alclad fuselage and peered into the ball turret. Walking around the wing, I stopped at the number four engine and put my hand on the prop. How many times, I wondered, had I helped pull these props through. Stooping, I went under the wing and past the number one and two engines. Taking one last look at the radio room window from the outside, I slowly worked my way around the horizontal stabilizer to the tail turret. Finally, with a lump in my throat, I soberly walked to where my wife waited.

⌘

The B-17 was called a Flying Fortress because of its fire power, not because of its ability to protect its crew. There was very little armor to do that. In most places the only thing between the crew and Mother Earth ... sometimes more than four miles below ... was a thin sheet of Alclad aluminum. As the aircraft struggled through acres of punishing flak, or was attacked by enemy fighters, there was no place to hide. She was all we had. If she went down we bailed out ... or went down with her.

Why, then, were the men who flew her so attached to her? The answer is; there was one thing about her we knew ... although many men were killed by flack or fighters, they had to practically blow her out of the sky to knock her down. She had an amazing ability to sustain unbelievable battle damage and still carry on. And she did her job like no other. She will always be something very special to me.

As we turned and walked past the hundreds of people of all ages now waiting to go through her, I thought … Oh the stories I could tell them of this once mighty aircraft.

1

*Detroit, Michigan, Sunday,
December 7, 1941*

TODAY AMERICANS WERE SHOCKED INTO REALITY. Until today, we thought we were safe from all the wars being waged overseas. After all, we were surrounded by vast oceans, and who would dare attack our invincible Navy and Air Force!

But in Hawaii, on December 7, 1941, the unthinkable happened. By the end of the day the backbone of our Navy was at the bottom of the sea; much of our Air Force was destroyed on the ground; and more than two thousand Americans were dead... *all in one day.*

Just about every American soberly sat by the radio as the news of the Japanese surprise attack on Pearl Harbor spread throughout the world. As most Americans, we were practically glued to the radio now. For the very first time, Americans had a sense of vulnerability.

On December 8, the United States declared war on Japan.

On December 11, Italy and Germany declared war on the United States.

It was apparent now that at least my eighteen-year-old brother Glen, and even I, at sixteen, most likely were going to war.

⌘

Detroit, Michigan,
Saturday, May 15, 1943

It wasn't much of a celebration, my eighteenth birthday. I found that being a male teenager in those trying times since 1941 was worrisome indeed. Every day something reminded us of the war. You couldn't escape it. Posters like, Uncle Sam's *I Want You,* and *A Slip of the Lip Sinks a Ship*, were everywhere. Among others, H. V. Kaltenborn, Edward R. Murrrow, Lowell Thomas and Walter Winchill, reminded the nation of the war by radio on a daily basis. The newspapers gave us a blow by blow description in print, while magazines and newsreels provided us with incredible pictures of destruction, and gruesome pictures of the war dead. You couldn't get away from it at the movies... if the main feature wasn't about the war, the newsreel was.

In all honesty I had no burning desire to fight the Germans, or the Japs... or anyone else for that matter. Seeing the movie All Quiet on the Western Front was enough for me, so I did not jump at the opportunity to enlist.

That did not mean I was unpatriotic, the fact of the matter is, I considered myself a patriot. Two of the men I admired the most in those days were Franklin Delano Roosevelt and Sir Winston Churchill. I did not agree with the America First people, who I suspected were

Pro Nazi. Deep down inside I believed that Hitler was an evil man, and he had to be stopped. So I registered for the draft, and hoped for the best. The best being that I would flunk my physical. But that scenario turned out to be wishful thinking. When I took my pre-induction physical in Detroit, I was classified 1A.

But, much to my surprise I was given the opportunity to join the Enlisted Reserve Corps. In so doing I was assured that I would not be called up for at least ninety days, and then I would be given my choice of services. I liked that. The longer I put it off the better. Who knows what could happen in ninety days. And by doing this, I could avoid the infantry, my last choice of the services. [Sorry guys, no offense intended.]

Then I quit my temporary job [nailing tops on boxes of roller bearings] and spent most of that ninety days relaxing around a community swimming pool with my younger brother, Wayne. Still fresh in my mind was the sad scene at the railroad station last January as the family said goodby to my older brother, Glen. Glen was now attending an air force cadet school learning how to fly. Soon I would be leaving, and if this war didn't end soon brother Wayne would probably follow. That would leave sister Joan the only sibling left at home.

My parents were worried sick about all this, but they had survived World War I, and the Great Depression, and they would survive this too.

August 24, 1943,
Detroit, Michigan

My ninety days ran out on the 24th of August, and from that day on my life would never be the same. That day I received my first telegram, it was from Uncle Sam, and was called *Special Orders No. 99*. I still have that original telegram. It reads:

> "Effective September 11, 1943, each of the above mentioned enlisted men of the Enlisted Reserve Corps is called to active duty and will proceed from the city mentioned above to Fort Custer, Michigan, reporting to the Commanding Officer, Recruit Reception Center thereat for Duty."

I, Robert Lee Thornton, serial number 36 876 569, was one of the above mentioned enlisted men. The city mentioned above was Detroit, and that telegram would propel me into the greatest human tragedy of our time.

2

Detroit, Michigan,
September 11, 1943

THIS WAS A BIG DAY FOR ME BECAUSE IT WAS THE DAY I EMBRACED MY FAMILY AND BOARDED A TRAIN BOUND FOR FORT CUSTER, MICHIGAN. I was on my way to join our Allies in the war against the Axis. As I did so, fifty-six nations were at war and it had become the bloodiest conflict in recorded history. The next twenty-eight months would seem like a lifetime to me, and for many others… it was.

In the coming months, I would witness incredible destruction and participate in frightening air battles the likes of which had never been seen before and will never be seen again. Battles in which huge air armadas fought their way to targets deep inside Germany.

We would be harassed by the Luftwaffe's highly maneuverable ME-109s, deadly FW-190s, and you could always count on plenty of what we called "Ack. Ack."[antiaircraft fire]. Later we saw the first jet fighters used in combat, the ME-262s. And last, the first and only manned rocket fighter, the ME-163 Komet, we called the Bat Plane.

The clear blue sky around me would fill with thousands of black polka dots called flak [exploding antiaircraft shells]. Bomb-laden aircraft would erupt in orange and red flames, only thick black smoke remaining as tons of burning debris and bodies hurtled earthward. I would count billowy white parachutes carrying comrades to an uncertain fate. These, and other horrors I am about to relate, make my hand tremble as I write... over a half century later.

Never having been more than two hundred miles from home before, I was now on my way into the great unknown, on this, my first train ride. Wallowing in self pity, I was convinced that I would never see my family again. With a lump in my throat and an ache in my heart, I settled back in my seat and listened to the unfamiliar, clickity-clack-clickity-clack, the trains big steel wheels made as they passed over the track.

We lumbered westward, through the city, past the warehouses, junkyards and suburbs. Picking up speed, we entered the rolling sunny hills of southern Michigan. The foliage was already starting to turn bright red and vivid yellow in preparation for October, the most beautiful month of the year in these parts. In other times I would have relished the view. Today, I hardly noticed it.

Hours later, the clickity-clack-clickity-clack, slowed. I looked out the window and saw the station in Battle Creek. This was it, from here I would go by bus to Fort Custer.

[Years later, I would learn that, also on this same day... September /11/1943... American airmen were looking out the windows of their B-17 Flying Fortresses as they landed at air base No. 109, called Podington Airdrome, in England. Upon

disembarking, they were greeted by a small RAF holding party who then turned the base over to them. These airmen were members of the 92nd Bomb Group of the Army's 8th Air Force. They had just arrived at their new home. Little did I know as I stepped from my train in Battle Creek that day, how this event, so far away, would affect my life.]

Fort Custer Reception Center, Fort Custer Michigan, September 12-13

At Fort Custer I underwent another physical examination. Standing in a room that resembled a high school gymnasium with several dozen other naked men, I was told to raise my left foot behind me. An army doctor examined my foot and whistled. "Hey Major, come look at this!" Another man came over behind me.

"Let's see the other foot, Soldier," the new man said. So I switched feet.

"Do those feet bother you?" the man asked.

"No Sir," I replied.

"You must want in this man's army awfully bad Soldier... those are the flattest feet I have ever seen." And with that, the new man turned and walked away.

Since I never knew that I had flat feet I was dumbstruck. The army was not a place I wanted to be. Why, I wondered, hadn't they picked this up in Detroit during my pre-induction physical? But for some reason, still unknown to me, I remained silent and said nothing to change the man's mind. That night, though, I unhappily lay in bed thinking of what I should have said. Nevertheless, the next morning I boarded a train bound for St. Louis. My destination was the basic training camp at Jefferson Barracks, Missouri.

Jefferson Barracks, Missouri, Monday, September 14

Everyone called Jefferson Barracks, "JB." It was a very old facility. Abraham Lincoln, while in the Illinois State Militia, was involved in the capture of Chief Black Hawk, who was incarcerated at "JB" in 1832.

While at "JB" I endured the typical rigors of basic training that have been so aptly depicted in multitudes of plays, movies and TV shows. We sang as we marched and we marched just about everywhere we went. In the morning we fell out for roll call before dawn and marched to breakfast. We marched to lunch and we marched to dinner. I went through the trials and tribulations with the drill sergeants, pulled KP [kitchen police], carried a back pack and rifle on the twenty mile hikes, went on the bivouacs, and played the war games.

That kind of stuff really makes a man out of a guy, right? Well... among other things, my eyebrows and lashes were singed and I almost went deaf one dark night when some *idiot* deliberately fired a blank in my face during a stupid war game. Then I spent fourteen days in the hospital with something like pneumonia after a bivouac in a cold, damp, mosquito infested forest next to the Mississippi River. But as they say... all's well that ends well. I was still alive.

In the process someone asked, "In what branch of the service do you wish to serve?" Without hesitating I replied, "The Air Corps." That's where brother Glen was and it sounded rather glamorous as compared to my other choices.

Subsequently, I was one of the thirty-six men of my group who took the mental and physical exam required by the Air Corps. On October 9, 1943, the names of the men who had passed that test were posted on our bulletin board. There were nineteen names on the list, and mine was one of them. Since the only openings in the Air Corps at that time were for Flight Engineer Gunners, and ROMGs [Radio Operator Mechanic Gunners] we could take our choice. I opted for the ROMG.

After completing basic training I received orders to report to the Army Air Forces Training Command for Radio Operator Mechanics at Scott Field, Illinois on December 23. So on the morning of the 23rd, I loaded my duffle bag onto an army bus and made the short trip to Scott Field, Illinois. As we passed through the main gate I felt a little better about my life. I was now a member of the United States Army Air Corps.

Scott Field, Illinois,
Thursday, December 23

Many things were taught at Scott Field. To graduate, a student had to have the ability to, among other things:

1. Maintain and repair all radio equipment on board his ship.
2. Encode, decode, and send and receive Morse Code messages on continuous wave frequencies [CW].
3. Render position reports.
4. Assist the navigator in taking fixes. And,
5. Maintain a log

Air to ground communications were an important part of our training, and I never will forget my first flight.

Most people who read this may think nothing of boarding an aircraft today, but in 1943 regular airlines were in their infancy. The accepted modes of transportation were trains, buses, cars and even horses were being used by some. There were few airline flights available and flying was expensive; it was considered a glamorous way to travel, used only by the wealthy.

Sitting in my barracks that evening after that flight, I felt very sentimental and took a pen in hand to express my emotions to the folks back home.

"I sit looking out a window into a dark and rainy night. Frank Sinatra is singing "Long Ago and Far Away" on the radio. The rain is forming tiny rivulets on the window panes. Red lights are blinking on the wingtips of landing aircraft and I can see the reflection of those lights mirrored on the dark wet runway."

Thanks to my father, who saved all of our war correspondence, I have before me another letter written that same night. Only this letter was written, Somewhere in the Atlantic, by brother Glen. Glen had not qualified as a pilot, but had recently graduated from an Aerial Navigation school and was now a 2nd Lieutenant.

His letter also tells of new and emotional experiences. It describes the trials and tribulations of a young serviceman aboard a ship at sea. Glen was on an ocean infested with German U-boats at a time in history when U-boats were sinking Allied ships in record numbers.

Although he didn't know it at the time, he was on his way to join the 457th Bomb Group of the Army's 8th Air

Corps at Glatton, England. He would fly his first combat mission over Europe as a navigator on a B-17 next month. A tour of duty at that time was thirty missions, but the average airman only survived fifteen. A sobering thought, indeed.

We had little time for recreation at Scott Field but we occasionally received week end passes. Another letter tells of my first blind date. It happened on Saturday, April 22nd.

Dick, a classmate from Charleston, Illinois, arranged the date through his girlfriend, a student at Eastern Illinois College. Dick had a car and drove. My date, from Danville, Illinois, was a stunning, beautiful blond. So beautiful, I felt bewitched. I had had very little experience dating back home, having foolishly been more interested in baseball and football than the opposite sex. The mere presence of this young lady made a bumbling idiot of me. Most of the time I was tongue-tied and acted like a dunce.

The ladies graciously treated us to a picnic in a nearby park and I somehow awkwardly struggled through the event. My date must have thought I was some kind of idiot. For months afterward I indulged in self punishment by mentally reviewing that date and telling myself how stupid I was, and what I *should* have said, and what I *should have done.*

⌘

On our return trip to Scott Field, the Illinois State Police pulled us over to the side of the road. Instead of coming to the car one of the troopers told us to get out with our hands up. And of course, we obeyed. I turned to face the police car behind us and saw the business end of a shotgun. This weapon, aimed at my chest, was held by a trooper crouched behind the hood of a squad car. Another trooper frisked us. When he found no weapons, he searched Dick's car, apologized and released us. He said a local bank had been robbed that day by two soldiers.

But now we arrived back at Scott Field five minutes late. You would think that five minutes was no big deal, right? Wrong. At least not in the army. Our commanding officer decided to make an example of us, or he just got out of the wrong side of the bed that morning. He used the 104th Article of War on us.

The 104th Article of War allows commanding officers to impose disciplinary action against persons of his command without the intervention of a court-martial. Disciplinary punishment authorized by this article may include admonition, a reprimand, withholding of privileges and extra fatigue.

This commanding officer not only admonished us, he reprimanded us, withheld the privilege of our next pass, and ordered us to do extra fatigue [KP]. In other words, he "threw the book" at us.

Some weeks later, while undergoing an overseas physical, I flunked the blood pressure part. Strangely, nobody mentioned my flat feet, but then, even more strangely, neither did I. My blood pressure was high, so I was told to go back to the barracks and do nothing but rest until tomorrow. But the next day it was still high. This time the doctor gave me similar orders and warned… *"you know, soldier, three times and you're out!"*

What! I thought. *One more time and I'm out'a here?* All that day, and most of that night I lay on my bunk staring at the ceiling, day dreaming of how I would spend the rest of my life. I thought of how happy my family would be to see me, and of all the money I would make in some defense plant in Detroit. Perhaps I could even go to college. *Hot-diggity-dog*, I thought. *I'm going home for sure this time!*

Snap… just like that I had forgotten about my newborn pride of passing that test and becoming an airman. Going home sounded much better to me than going to war.

When I reported the next day, a captain greeted me. I had been seeing a second lieutenant. The captain showed me to a patient room and told me to lie down on the examining room table, then he left. I was there a long time. It was a little chilly that morning but the table was next to the window and the sun felt so good… I fell asleep. As I woke up, I saw the captain rolling up his blood pressure cuff. "Congratulations soldier, you passed," he said. He never told me what my blood pressure was, but he did say something about 'white coat syndrome.'

With my hopes of going home dashed, I reluctantly decided on another strategy, something I read in a Norman Vincent Peale book. "Make the best of it"… excel in this class and become the best dammed Radio Operator Mechanic Gunner in the Air Corps.

In another letter home, written on May 16, 1944, I tell of how I celebrated my nineteenth birthday in St. Louis with Rose, a very pretty brunette. While at Scott Field, I spent most of my weekends with Rose and her family. She had a large fun-loving family and they took me in as if I were one of their own. We sat around on hot Sunday afternoons drinking beer, Rose's father worked for Anheuser-Busch. Although I did not turn twenty-one until after the war, and could not legally be served alcoholic beverages at the time, I was never refused a drink while in uniform.

Rose introduced me to beautiful Forest Park. We saw the Operetta "The Open Road," at the Municipal Opera Theater celebrating its 26th season in the park that year. I still have the program after all these years.

St. Louis was growing on me and I thought I was falling in love with the young lady. Just as I was about to lose my virginity, July 1, graduation day, rolled around, and I had to say goodbye to Rose. [Believe it or not, kids, it was a different world back then.]

Rose and I corresponded for a long time afterward, but as happened to so many war time romances, Rose started telling me about this great guy she met and the letters eventually stopped. The flame was out.

About 30 percent of my class had washed out, including Len, a family friend from Roseville, Michigan. In order to graduate you had to be able to take twenty words per minute of Morse Code. If you failed, you washed back one class. It was the old three times and you're out thing.

Anyway, my reward for graduating was a promotion to corporal, and on Independence Day, July 4, we graduates boarded a train bound for an aerial gunnery school near Yuma, Arizona. As we left, Len wished me well as he waited to give the Morse Code class a second try.

The next time I heard from Len, I had about five missions under my belt. He had flunked out two more times and was on his way to a gunnery school. No more ROMG for him. Not a very smart guy, huh? Here *I* was, a Tech Sergeant, making all that money [my base pay, flying pay and overseas pay] and *Len* was still a buck private going to school. As it turned out, he never even got to see the world like I did. In fact, he never did make it overseas. [*I know what you're thinking. Don't say it. Just remember Norman Vincent Peale.*]

⌘

That train ride to Yuma is a ride I would like to forget. It took the southern route, south through Missouri and Arkansas. At Texarkana, the train turned westward and slowly chugged across Texas. I thought we would never get out of Texas. Then we went through New Mexico, and all the way across Arizona to the small town of Yuma. We were on that train four days and nights. When we could sleep, we slept in our seats. Temperatures reached over one-hundred degrees most days, with no air-conditioning. All windows were open all of the time. Smoke from the coal fired steam-engine blew back through the open windows. We were soon covered with soot and the fumes were awful. Our only water was drinking water. A converted box car served as our mess hall and we stopped three times a day at sidings to eat. We ate from mess kits on the railroad sidings.

Sometimes the train moved so slow, pranksters actually jumped off and ran alongside just for a lark.

The old Gila trail followed the Gila River for many miles across Arizona. Little did I know as our train chugged alongside that river that I was passing the grave site of my Great-Great Grandfather, Sam Thornton.

Sometime in 1850, forty-two-year-old Sam Thornton was in a wagon train on his way to the gold fields in California, when, according to one of his partners, he "sickened and died on the Gila Trail and was buried near the river under a Cottonwood tree."

[My Great-Great-Grandmother, Barbara, never believed that story, she thought his partners murdered him for his share of the money. However he died, it was a shame. After a very long grueling trip, he was so close to his destination. California was just miles away on the other side of the Colorado River at Yuma.]

Yuma, Arizona,
Saturday, July 8, 1944

When we finally arrived at our destination, the Yuma Army Air Force base, we were covered with sweat and grime, desperately needed a shave and smelled worse than a football locker room in the summertime.

The base was just east of Yuma, in the desert, but after that terrible trip the desert seemed like heaven. Small open air tents on wood platforms made up our barracks. We rolled up the canvas sides of the tents and used mosquito netting instead.

Four double bunk beds and eight foot lockers were in each tent. Latrines and showers were in a separate building. And this was the only base I ever saw that came with the luxury of an Olympic size swimming pool.

As we marched around in temperatures of 120 degrees or more, we sang a popular song of the day, *Only Mad Dogs and Englishmen go out in the Noonday Sun!*

However, evenings were cool and usually required a blanket. The first man in the latrine in the morning occasionally found a rattlesnake curled up on the floor. Little critters, sometimes scorpions, liked to hide in our shoes at night. We always shook our shoes out before we put them on.

The armament on air force heavy bombers in 1944 consisted of air-cooled fifty caliber machine guns. We had to know this weapon like the back of our hand. That meant field stripping and reassembling it while blindfolded. We used shotguns to fire at skeet from the beds of stake trucks traveling in the opposite direction. An elaborate simulation device enabled us to fire at phantom fighters on a giant wraparound screen.

One day, we went up in a B-17 and fired at bed sheets staked out on the desert floor below. Dust kicked up by our slugs revealed our accuracy. The temperature inside the aircraft, just a few hundred feet off the ground, was like an oven. The heat rising off the desert floor created turbulence causing the plane to pitch and lurch. These conditions created an ideal atmosphere for airsickness. I don't know why, but everyone got sick that day but me. Even the instructor got sick. Fortunately, to this day I have been spared the agony of airsickness and seasickness.

On another hot day in August, we went out on the desert to fire the fifty caliber machine gun at moving targets mounted on railroad tracks laid out like a huge race track. Only one student could fire at any given time. When ready to fire the student mounted the gun on a stationary two-inch pipe. After firing he moved the gun to folding tables standing nearby for cleaning. These guns were air-cooled and normally fired at high altitudes from planes traveling at high speeds at temperatures less than sixty degrees below zero. Even under those circumstances, after firing about fifteen rounds, the barrels got very hot. On the desert floor, not moving, they got much hotter.

On that particular day I had fired and was cleaning my gun. When the last man fired, I heard his GI shoes grind on the desert floor behind me as he approached my table, then I heard the gun go off. The man had committed a cardinal sin. He had not cleared his gun and the round left in the chamber had just "cooked-off."

In a split second, pandemonium broke loose. Blood was splattered everywhere. I saw blood on my fatigues and thought I was hit. But it was somebody else's blood. Seven men lay on the ground around me writhing and moaning. As it turned out three were seriously wounded, the other wounds were minor. Fortunately, everyone survived.

Close examination revealed that the slug had hit one of the table legs on *my* table. The legs were galvanized steel pipes. The slug and leg shattered sending the fragments flying like a hand grenade… I had just dodged my first bullet.

There were times when we just went flying for pleasure, mainly to escape the oppressive heat. We loaded a case of beer on the plane [it would keep cool at higher altitudes] and took off. I found flying over the Grand Canyon at sunset a particularly rewarding flight and a truly spectacular sight.

⌘

On Saturday, August 26, 1944, most of our class graduated. I was now a full-fledged ROMG. I also received sergeant stripes, Air Crew wings [I still have them] and orders to report to Lincoln, Nebraska for assignment to an air combat crew. I had ten days, called a delay-en-route, in which to report.

Lincoln, Nebraska, Tuesday, September 5

Traveling to Lincoln, by way of Detroit, was a hectic trip. Detroit is not exactly on the way to Lincoln when coming from Yuma. In those days we traveled by bus and train. There were no superhighways, and buses seemed to stop in every little hamlet along the way. Trains weren't much better. Consequently, I was only in Detroit a few days. This would be the last time I would see my parents until the war was over. This separation was far more emotional than the last, since everyone knew that I was on my way overseas.

Back at Lincoln I was processed and assigned to a combat crew, then ordered to report to an air base near Ardmore, Oklahoma.

Ardmore, Oklahoma, September 13

It had taken one year and two days for me to reach this point in time. Most of France, Belgium and Luxembourg had been liberated by Allied troops, and I knew that we would be training as a bomber crew for several more months. When I arrived in Ardmore on September 13, 1944, and met the other eight men that made up our nine man crew, I was thrilled. We were about to embark on a great adventure together, and I was excited.

The following men appear in our crew picture taken in front of aircraft #2854, the "Arkansas Rambler."

Top Left to right:

(1) Lt. Henry (Hank) Lapinski. Hank was our pilot and the airplane commander. He was charged with all the duties and responsibilities of a command post. That meant that he was responsible for the safety and efficiency of the crew at all times, not just while flying, but twenty-four hours a day of every day he was in command.

(2) Lt. Glenn [Whitey] Holsinger. Copilot and executive officer. As second in command he was the pilot's chief assistant, understudy, and strong right arm. Copilots had to be qualified to take over the crew at any given time.

(3) Flight Officer Theodore [Ted] Fossberg. Bombardier. When attacked by fighters he also manned the chin turret in the nose.

(4) Flight Officer Robert [Bob] Johnson. Navigator. Bob was required to direct the flight of the aircraft from its departure to destination and return. He also manned the two flexible guns in the nose.

Bottom Row left to right:

(5) Corporal Howard [Les] Brazier. Waist gunner.

(6) Corporal Mal Abrams. Tail gunner.

(7) Sergeant Robert Thornton. Radio Operator. I maintained a log, rendered position reports, obtained navigational fixes and kept the various radio sets tuned and in good operating condition. I also manned the unattended waist gun when under attack by enemy fighters.

(8) Corporal George Waldschmidt. Ball Turret gunner.

(9) Sergeant George Jaeger. Engineer. Participated in preflight inspections and played a vital role in the cockpit, especially during takeoffs and landings.

Since there were two Bob's and two George's on the crew, it was decided that the engineer would be called "Jaeger," and I would be called "Thornton."

At Ardmore, I also became friends with Tom Shanahan. Tom was from the west side of Detroit. Although billeted in separate barracks, we frequently met in the day room where we discussed current events and wrote letters home. We also relaxed in the Enlisted Men's Club and Post theater.

Weather permitting, we spent most of our waking hours flying. We practiced landings, day and night, for hours upon hours. When on simulated combat missions, we flew as far away as Galveston, Texas. Real fighters attacked us in mock battles. Together, the crew practiced ditching procedures and attended combat seminars.

An incident occurred one night as we were returning to Ardmore from a night flight over Texas. I mention it now because of a similar episode that would happen later. As we should have been approaching the base, Hank unsuccessfully tried to raise the tower. Over the intercom, he asked the navigator what was wrong. Bob gave him another heading and we flew on. Later Hank called Bob again and said that he still couldn't raise the tower. In a few minutes, with no response from Bob, Hank called me and told me to get him a "fix" [a radio operator's means of obtaining a heading.] I presumed we were lost. Hank sounded highly agitated.

The pilot talked to the tower and other aircraft over an ultra high frequency command set. It utilized what is called "line of sight" transmission. Ultra high frequencies go right on through the ionosphere and are not reflected back to earth as low frequencies are. Therefore, the ranges of ultra high frequencies are severely limited. Low frequencies travel around the earth by bouncing off the ionosphere, back to earth and out to the ionosphere, again and again and again.

The radio operator could communicate with just about anyone in the world on CW using Morse Code. Both systems were necessary on heavy bombers in those days.

This was my first opportunity to send a real message. Using Morse code, I quickly got my man at Ardmore, told him I needed a QDM [our code for a "fix"], then held my sending key down for one minute. The tower shot a "fix" on me and then gave me a heading. By rotating his antenna in a circle and monitoring my signal, the man in the tower could determine our direction, Ergo, "fix." He could then give me a correct heading to the base. The whole operation took just a couple of minutes, I gave the new heading to Hank, and we were on our way back to the base.

⌘

In a recent letter from home, I learned that brother Glen had beaten the odds and had safely completed his tour of thirty missions. He was now back in the States for reassignment. You can imagine my surprise when, with no forewarning, he showed up at Ardmore. He was on a delay-en-route and stopped in to see me. Our paths had crossed before, we had met in Chicago, Houston and Dallas. But our meeting in Ardmore was most unusual. The day Glen dropped in on me we were scheduled for a training flight that I couldn't get out of. Hank solved the problem by suggesting that Glen come along with us, and he did. On the front cover of this book, you will find a picture of my brother and me, taken just before we boarded the aircraft that day!.

Hank was the only married man on his crew, and his wife, Betty, was staying with him near the base. Shortly before our overseas flight, Hank took the whole crew to dinner in Ardmore, and that's where I first met Betty. The second time I met her was in 1995, fifty one years later, when Hank and Betty paid my wife and I a visit at our home in Florida. The four of us have been meeting regularly ever since.

Lincoln, Nebraska,
December 10

Now ready for the "big show," the crew returned to Lincoln in preparation for overseas duty. Many things had to be done. Immunization records were updated [different shots were required for different theaters]. We were asked to turn in our Khakis [tan cotton uniforms] and were issued new ODs [olive-drab] woolen uniforms, down sleeping bags, new duffle bags, and a garment bag. I received a "Hack" watch. Radio operators logged all messages and "Hack" watches were needed to accurately record the time.

Although our destination was unknown to us, because of the ODs and cold weather gear, we knew we were *not* going to the Pacific. With everything "ship shape," we spent the next few days doing shake down flights in a brand-new B17G we were to fly overseas. On December 19 we completed those flights and spent our last night in Lincoln, Nebraska.

Grenier Field, New Hampshire, December 20

On the morning of December 20, we boarded our aircraft in Lincoln and took off. Our destination was Grenier Field, New Hampshire. Late that afternoon we landed at Grenier. We would spend the night there while our aircraft was being refueled. After an early breakfast, on December 21 we attended a briefing session for a flight to Gander, Newfoundland. At that briefing Hank received sealed orders to be opened only after we were in the air on our way to Gander. Once in the air, headed for Gander, Hank opened his orders and announced that we were on our way to the ETO [European Theater of Operations]. We would be operating out of the UK [United Kingdom].

Gander, Newfoundland, Thursday, December 21

It was snowing when we landed in Gander, and very cold. We were to spend the night there. The wind was so strong Hank had the crew tie the wings down. He also wanted one man to stay with the aircraft at all times. We would take turns.

Two other brand new B17s landed that day and it was expected that we would all take off for the UK in the morning. Our accommodations at Gander were excellent. This base had been used by civilians ferrying planes to England before the U.S. entered the war. I was surprised to learn that many of the civilian pilots in those days were female.

On the morning of the 22nd, we awoke to a blinding snow storm and the weather man predicted more of the same for the next day. Our flight was put on hold until conditions improved. The storm continued into Christmas Eve, with no sign of letting up. I spent my second Christmas in the armed forces at Gander.

Pulling guard duty in the aircraft was boring, but warm. Thanks to our new down sleeping bags. The aircraft creaked as the wind howled and strained at the ropes holding it down. As the storm went on into the 26th and 27th of December, we had plenty of time to reflect on what was going on, on the other side of the Atlantic.

Many things had happened in the ETO since September 23, most of them good. Up until December 16, a few days before we landed at Gander, things were going so well for the Allies that some Generals were predicting an early end to the war. But on December 16, the war took an ominous turn. Hitler unleashed a counter offensive in the Ardennes with his 5th Panzer Division. They quickly broke through the American lines and thus began the greatest battle ever fought by American armies. Hitler called it *Die Wacht Am Rhein* [*The Watch on the Rhine*]. The Allies called it *The Battle of the Bulge.*

Our armies were suffering terrible losses and the allies feared that another Dunkirk could be at hand. [More Americans died in *The Battle of the Bulge* than General MacArthur lost in retaking *all* of the islands in the Pacific.] As we sat in Gander on December 27, things looked very grim. The 82nd Airborne was surrounded at Bastogne and when asked to surrender General McAuliffe made his now famous reply, *Nuts.* There was no doubt in my mind now, *I was going to see action.*

3

IN 1919, JUST SIX YEARS BEFORE I WAS BORN, TWO ENGLISHMEN TOOK OFF FROM THE BRITISH ISLES AND LANDED IN NEWFOUNDLAND, THUS BECOMING THE FIRST MEN TO FLY THE ATLANTIC. In 1927, when I was two years old, Charles A. Lindbergh took off [*solo*] from New Jersey in the Spirit of St. Louis, and thirty-three hours later landed in Paris. Now, just *seventeen* years after Lindbergh's flight, we too were going to fly the Atlantic. Of course, many others had done it in the meantime. But to think of how far mankind had come in such a short time, was to me, mind boggling.

On the morning of December 28, 1944, we were cleared to take off. As we taxied to the runway Hank told us that our next stop would be Belfast, Northern Ireland. We were on our way to become members of the U.S. Army's 8th Air Force.

How coincidental this was I thought. Just a few months ago brother Glen was flying combat missions in B-17s in the 8th Air Force. Only weeks ago we had flown a practice mission together. Now Glen was safely stateside and I was on my way to continue where he left off. Could our family be so lucky to have *both* of us survive? I wondered what the odds were.

The weather had improved but was still ugly. Although the runway was plowed, a huge bank of snow bordered each side. Twenty-seven airmen showed up for breakfast that morning and now all three crews were about to take off. We knew the weather was bad, but as we slowly lumbered down the wind swept runway, we had no idea that we were flying into a storm even worse than the storm we were leaving behind. Our wheels left the ground, the snow-covered terrain slipped behind us, and we slowly climbed out over the dark raging Atlantic.

As the morning passed the weather grew worse and we soon lost sight of the other two aircraft. We were bucking a strong and turbulent headwind, and Hank first tried to climb over it. But we had no oxygen and the storm was too high. Then he dropped down as low as he dared and the plane struggled on, hour after hour after hour. Conditions were so bad I wondered how anyone in his right mind would have cleared us to take off back in Gander.

I had never seen an ocean, and the sight of rogue waves higher than ten story buildings astonished me. Looking down at that whirling fury of water made me wonder how any ship could survive down there. Now I was glad that I had not done what my father had in WW I, and joined the navy.

But, after eleven hours and twenty minutes of wrestling with that spanking new shiny aircraft, Hank and Whitey put it down safely in Belfast. We disembarked in drizzling rain. The temperature was in the fifties. I was surprised that the grass was still green.

[Fifty-seven years later, over lunch in a restaurant in Punta Gorda, Florida, Hank recalled how grueling and exhausting that flight was on him and Whitey. He

*said that he had never seen a storm like that before…
or since. With no oxygen, the storm had forced him
down much too low for comfort. He agreed with me,
that the sea below was frightening. It was a flight, he
said, that he will never forget.]*

4

~~~~~~

"Somewhere in England,"
Thursday, December 29

AT AN AIRBASE IN BELFAST WE ATTENDED AN INDOCTRINATION COURSE. We learned that a tour of duty was now *thirty-five* missions. A tour had gone from twenty-five, to thirty, and was now thirty-five missions.

While in the United Kingdom [UK] we must obey English law and we were told how that law differed from ours. And as official representatives of the United States Army Air Force in a foreign country, we were expected to act accordingly… as *gentlemen.*

We attended lectures on many subjects; ranging from sex to eating food in an English restaurant. From this day on we were to obey a strict security code. All of our correspondence would be censored. Military activities would be discussed with *no* one. Nor could we reveal our whereabouts. Our letters would start with "Somewhere in England."

We were lectured on what to expect if we had to bail out over enemy territory. Carrying wallets, or any kind of identification was strictly taboo. Once on the ground we were to strip to our ODs, rip off all insignias and bury or hide anything that could identify us. Our ODs would not attract attention because many people in Europe were walking around in ODs we were told. However, we would have to do something about our shoes. Europeans wore black shoes and our brown shoes would easily give us away. We must find some way of blackening or muddying our shoes.

When eating we would have to eat like Europeans. Europeans always keep their fork in one hand and their knife in the other. They never switch their knife and fork as we do. When smoking a cigarette Europeans let it dangle from their lips even while talking. The only time they remove it is to throw it away.

We were told the story of how an English spy on the Continent was apprehended by an alert German soldier. The spy gave himself away by inadvertently looking first to his *right* while crossing a street. Traffic in England flows in opposite directions from that on the Continent. People there instinctively look to their *left* first as we do in the U.S.

Our last day in Belfast was also the last day of 1944. It was New Years Eve and that evening we ushered in the new year by attending a dance held on the base. Local girls were bussed in for the occasion and for the first time we met our Allies. That is, the female gender.

We awoke the next morning to a new year. Dawn was breaking and the rain had stopped. It was going to be a sunny but cold day. After an early breakfast and a short drive we boarded our first British train. Our aircraft stayed, it had to be modified for the ETO.

British trains always fascinated me with their shrill whistle and cozy, intimate, compartments [most of them are antiques now]. Traveling on these trains in the coming months became part of a romantic relationship with the Isles that I will never forget. I immediately fell in love with this picturesque land.

We disembarked from the train at a port on the Irish Sea and boarded a ferry. After a very rough voyage across that cold body of water we docked and were driven to another train.

Podington Airdrome, Bedfordshire, England, Monday, January 1, 1945

This was a very exciting day in our lives, we had just completed a very difficult crossing of the Atlantic and delivered a million dollar aircraft all in one piece. We had been made welcome in a foreign country and at long last were nearing our destination. Before this day was over, we would join the major leagues. For better or worse, our mettle would soon be tested doing the real thing.

Our second train ride ended in the city of Wellingborough, where we found a GI personnel carrier waiting for us. The driver carefully picked his way through the town and then took to the typical narrow roads that meander through the English countryside. Except for the pines, the trees and shrubs were barren of foliage. Patches of snow spotted the brown fields and green lawns. We passed through several villages and hamlets with quaint homes, shops, pubs and inns. Their narrow picturesque cobblestone streets slowed our truck to a crawl. I never saw a frame building in England, not even a barn. And there were few lawns in the cities. The entrances to most shops, pubs, homes and other buildings were right off the sidewalk next to the street.

We passed a church in the small village of Podington, and soon came upon an old mansion called Henwick

House. Just ahead, where two roads converged, we came to a guardhouse and gate. A large sign over the gate read: 92nd BOMB GROUP (H), HOME OF FAME'S FAVORED FEW. [The H meant, heavy bombardment.]

This was our destination. We were at Podington Airdrome in Bedfordshire. [In the states we referred to them as air bases, not airdromes. From now on I will refer to the field at Podington as an air base.] The small community of Podington is not far from, among others, Wellingborough, Wollaston, Bozeat, Northhampton, Rushden and Bedford.

Moments after passing through the main gate, we passed a bull penned in a large field. On the far side of the field there appeared to be a mess hall. I remember passing a farmhouse where a woman was hanging out laundry. Soon we stopped at a building bearing a sign that read 92nd BOMB GROUP HEADQUARTERS. In the distance I could see the control tower and other buildings.

This was all new to me. Air bases in the States were neatly laid out with perpendicular streets forming rectangular blocks, like in a city. Everything near the flight line and barracks were two story frame buildings. The only things that resembled the air bases I knew were the runways, hangers and tower.

Podington Air Base resembled a farm for a very good reason. Foremost, the use of the land for farming helped feed a population experiencing a severe food shortage. With air bases laid out in this manner, every available acre of land was in use to produce food. Secondly, the barracks and buildings were scattered in nearby clusters of trees. This made it more difficult for German aircraft to find them.

"Fame's Favored Few," the oldest group in the ETO, consisted of four squadrons, the 325th, 326th, 327th and

407th. On most missions, three of the four squadrons would put up twelve B-17s for a total of thirty-six. The fourth squadron was usually on standby.

This group was first organized at MacDill Field, Florida in 1942. Then, for operational training, they moved to the Sarasota-Bradenton Air Base [now the Sarasota-Bradenton International Airport]. In August of that year they made a nonstop flight from Gander, Newfoundland, to Scotland. The group flew its first mission from Bovington, England. They later moved to Alconbury in January of 1943. In September 1943, they moved again, this time to Podington.

Our crew was assigned to the 325th squadron under the command of Lieutenant Colonel Albert L. Cox, Jr. Our squadron was symbolized by the comic strip character Ally Oop, riding a tiger and brandishing a weapon resembling a stone club. I later proudly wore this symbol in the form of a patch sewn to the breast of my leather A2 jacket. I still have that original patch.

A cluster of Nissen huts, all but hidden in a grove of trees about a mile from the flight line, made up the 325th squadron. These low one story buildings housed the squadron headquarters, orderly room, latrines and barracks. All were now practically empty. The 325th was flying a mission today.

An orderly took us to our assigned hut. When I entered, I noticed a blue haze near the ceiling. The pot bellied "cherry" stove in the middle of the room was just smoldering. The cold, damp, room reeked of stale cigar and cigarette butts, woolen uniforms, overcoats, socks and underwear. To my left was a door to the only private room in the hut, occupied by the barrack's chief. Facing me was a long aisle with double bunk beds on each side except for the area around the stove. One foot locker was in front of each double bunk and another was against the wall. One for the man in the lower bunk and one for the man in the upper. On the far end of the room was another door leading outside.

Nude calendar girls by the famous artists Petty and Varga, as well as scantily clad photographs of girls adorned every available space on the walls. There were five empty bunks scattered about the room. The orderly told us to take our pick and make ourselves at home. As I scanned the room I thought, *It's not bad, it sure beats a fox hole.*

We had arrived in the UK during the worst winter in English recorded history. Air operations had been curtailed considerably. But not today, unfortunately. Unfortunately, because today, New Years day, 1945, was the day Hitler had chosen for an operation he called *Der Grosse Schlag* [*The Great Blow*]. We were completely unaware as we boarded our train that morning, that a great air battle had just begun on the other side of the English Channel. For months Luftwaffe generals had been assembling thousands of fighters and hoarding fuel and ammunition preparing for an operation they called *Herman.* This operation, a defensive one, was designed to eliminate American bombers from German skies, once and for all.

But, Hitler, as he had done so many times in the past, overruled his generals. Over their futile protests he canceled operation *Herman,* and hoping to bail out his stalling *Watch on the Rhine,* ordered this amassed arsenal to strike *Der Grosse Schlag.* That morning the 8th Air force flew into a hornet's nest. More than one thousand ME-109s and FW-190s attacked allied tactical air bases in Holland, Belgium and France. For the second time in two weeks [the first being The Battle of the Bulge] the allies had been taken by surprise. Many fighters and fighter bombers on the Continent were destroyed on the ground or just as they were taking off.

In retrospect, Hitler's intervention in operation *Herman* saved many lives of U.S. bomber crews. [New Years day being an exception.] In his *Great Blow,* Germany lost many of its top fighter pilots who could have been far more effective defending German skies. While the allies lost many planes on the ground, and some bomber crews, they lost very few fighter pilots. Planes could be replaced, but the pilots could not.

⌘

After eating our first meal at our new home, like magnets, we were drawn to the line to watch the group return from today's mission. Everyone had seen the documentary film *Memphis Belle,* but this was the real thing.

A large crowd was gathering near the control tower for the event. The railing of the observation deck was lined with high-ranking officers. Some were scanning the horizon through field glasses. Looking out over the field, I could see acres of hardstands [large cement circular parking places for planes] scattered in a huge half moon shape between the tower and the runways. These hardstands were connected to a network of roads leading to the runways, called perimeter strips. Some B-17s sat out there now, those of the standby squadron. There were three runways, numbered 1, 2, and 3. Number 1 being the main runway and the longest.

Every plane had a large white "B" on a black triangle painted on the dorsal fin [vertical part of the tail]. Of the three divisions of heavy bombers in the 8th Army Air

Force, the black triangle identified the First Division. The white "B" identified the 92ⁿᵈ Bomb Group. The first division was divided into Wings. The 92ⁿᵈ Bomb Group was part of the 40ᵗʰ CBC Wing.

Ground crews waited in jeeps near the line. Ambulances and fire trucks waited on the perimeter strip near the tower. All eyes focused on the eastern horizon where the group would first appear. Soon tiny silver specks glistening in the rays of a setting sun announced their arrival, and we heard the low rumble of many engines. The rumble grew louder and louder as they approached. They were in a modified "box" formation, coming in at about 1,500 feet. When they neared, the Group Leader peeled off and started a *three-sixty* [three hundred and sixty degree turn] into the landing pattern. One by one, others followed. While the lead squadron landed, the other two squadrons did a *three-sixty* around the field. The second time around the next squadron peeled off, while the third went around one more time.

Now the first plane, the Group Leader, was landing. With a screech the two huge tires protested with puffs of white burning rubber as they hit the concrete. The bristling giant bounced and hit again. This time the aircraft settled down and smoothly sped toward the far end of the runway. As it turned and started to taxi up the perimeter strip, the second, the deputy lead, was rolling halfway down the runway and a third plane was just about to hit. Others, as far as the eye could see, were strung out like steps on a spiral staircase.

After the Group Leader landed, we started counting. There was a lull after thirty-two, it looked like four were missing. After a few minutes, an officer with field glasses on the flight deck pointed to the east, and we soon saw a straggler. Daylight was fading fast as the aircraft let down with one engine gone. As his wheels touched down, another straggler appeared not far behind. The newcomer was coming in with only two engines. As he approached the runway, a red flare streaked from the stricken aircraft and curled downward. This meant there were wounded on board. Before her tires hit the runway, ambulances and fire trucks were racing alongside. Medics were boarding the aircraft as it stopped. Seconds later they off loaded a crewman and the ambulance sped away. As it turned out, the man was the engineer and he was already dead with a piece of shrapnel buried deep in his head.

Only thirty-four planes landed that day. The returning airmen reported being attacked by many enemy fighters. We later learned that an aircraft from the 407th exploded over the target and another, from the 326th, made a forced landing in France with three crewmen wounded. That day the 92nd lost one aircraft, nine men were missing and one man was known dead. Also, three men were wounded and many aircraft had sustained severe battle damage. This was our initiation to "Fame's Favored Few."

On the long, silent, walk back to our barracks that day, I believe we were all deep in thought. As for me, I was profoundly affected by what I had just witnessed… something had changed in me. I no longer thought of myself as a teenager. I had just become a man. I was suddenly proud of my uniform. Proud to be in the Air Force. Proud, and lucky, I thought, to be in this bomb group. And if I got out of this alive or not, I knew I had made the right decisions and done the right thing.

⌘

Both sides suffered heavy losses on New Years Day, 1945. And now it was reported that Air Force General Spaatz envisioned a war that would continue into autumn. More discouraging news greeted us in the morning. More than thirty enlisted ground personnel of the 92ⁿᵈ had been issued rifles, and were on their way to the Continent to help repulse the "Bulge." And if things got worse, we were told, ground crews and gunners would be next. The Allies were determined to do everything necessary to prevent another Dunkirk.

Later in the week I was in for a pleasant surprise. While looking for a place to sit in the mess hall, I spotted Tom Shanahan. Tom hadn't seen me, so I casually walked to his table and sat beside him. A big Irish grin spread over his face when he saw me. He had just arrived that morning, he said. Lt. Paul's crew had been assigned to the 327ᵗʰ Squadron.

On January 8, Mel, a radio operator in the bunk next to mine, failed to return from the day's mission. His plane was last seen going down over France. However, a few days later he showed up in good health. His plane had gone into a dive and then broke up. Luckily he had his chest pack chute on and simply pulled the rip cord.

In the meantime, weather permitting, we were busy flying practice missions over the Wash and attending aircraft identification classes. The old saying, "practice makes perfect," is axiomatic in the armed forces.

At the same time we were gradually becoming familiar with our new environment. An important part of that process was the "Liberty Run." GI personnel carriers provided a regular bus service to Northampton, called "Liberty Runs." In our free time, we were permitted to come and go as we pleased.

Owning a bicycle was a necessity. We used bicycles to get around the base and to visit the many small villages in the area. This soon became one of my favorite pastimes. I enjoyed drinking the warm "mild and bitters" draft beer and playing darts with the local townspeople.

Two mishaps struck the 92nd on January 10. First, an aircraft in the 327th was badly damaged over the target but made it to France. Then one of its engines started to "run away" and because of a misunderstanding, the navigator, bombardier and waist gunner, bailed out. However, the pilot crash landed the aircraft with no casualties.

The second occurred in the 325th and involved my barracks mate, Mel, again. His aircraft lost all four engines over the target. The pilot was able to restart one engine long enough to drop his bombs and make it to friendly territory. He then told the crew to prepare for a crash landing. But the waist gunner, only a few hundred feet off the ground, bailed out. His chute never opened and he was killed instantly. All other crew-members survived and returned home. Mel told me that his crew-mate must have panicked. He said everyone should have known they were too low to bail out.

We had only been members of the 92nd for ten days now and the group had lost four aircraft and eleven men. We did not have calculators in those days but it didn't take a mathematical genius to figure out that, at that rate, we would lose the equivalent of the *whole* group in about three months. And we hadn't flown our first mission yet. But that would soon change. On January 20, our names appeared on the alert list for the first time. Tomorrow we would fly our first mission.

5

THE LASTTIME I LOOKED AT MY PRACTI-CALLY BRAND NEW GOVERNMENT ISSUE HACK WATCH, I BELIEVE IT WAS ALMOST THREE-THIRTY, AND I KNEW THE ORDERLY WOULD BE WAKING US SOON.

Laying in my bunk, staring at the ceiling, my life seemed to be flashing before me. I wandered in and out of a semi-dream world. At one time I was back in Detroit, making a baseball out of a golf ball. I wound rubber bands around the golf ball and then wrapped it in friction tape. It was during the Great Depression. My father was out of work and we were on welfare. We couldn't afford things like baseballs, bats and gloves. All the boys in the neighborhood collected pop bottles, papers, and scrap metal to turn into cash to buy a bat, and when that broke, we broke all rules of safety and nailed it together then taped it.

Then I was in grade school and kids were making fun of my welfare shoes. Another time we were laying around the living room floor listening to "The Lone Ranger," "The Shadow," or "Amos 'n' Andy" on the radio, while mom was ironing in the dining room. Then it was Sunday morning and we were on the living room floor again, only now we were reading the funnies…

"Dick Tracy," "Flash Gordon," " Li'l Abner" and "Terry and the Pirates." Dad was always sitting in *his* overstuffed chair reading the news. Luckily, brother Glen had a paper route and he sometimes had a paper left over.

On a hot summer day we were sitting on the front steps waiting for the bells of the Good Humor man. I had a Liberty magazine route, and between my brother and me, we somehow managed to sometimes scrape up enough change for a treat.

Half awake, a sadness came over me as I saw the family gathered around the dining room table at dinner time on holidays. It seemed like only yesterday. But now, in a few hours I would be on my way to some town deep inside Germany. Perhaps I would make it through this mission, I thought, but certainly not *thirty-five*. I finally fell asleep, convinced I would never see my family again.

6

IN ROUND FIGURES THE B-17G WAS 75 FEET LONG AND HAD A WINGSPAN OF 104 FEET. With no load it weighed in at about 38,000 pounds. Its maximum speed was 302 MPH at 25,000feet. Its cruising speed was 160 MPH. With no bomb load it had a maximum range of 3,700 miles and a service ceiling of 35,000 feet. It could carry as much as 20,000 pounds of bombs.

The armament in January 1945, consisted of twelve fifty-caliber air-cooled machine guns. There were four turrets with two guns in each turret. The "chin" turret, in the nose, was manned by the bombardier when under attack. The "top" turret, just behind the cockpit, was manned by the engineer. The "ball" turret gunner was slung under the belly, and the last turret was manned by the tail gunner.

The big difference between the B-17G, and the old model B-17F was: the "F" had no "chin turret." The Luftwaffe shot down many B-17Fs by attacking head on, at 12 O'clock. They fired as they came in, then veering off just in time to avoid a collision. It's easy to identify the "F" model [as seen in the movie "12 O'clock High"] because they had no "chin turrets." The main reason

Boeing developed the "G" model was to add the chin turret to discourage "head on" attacks.

Turrets were much more effective than flexible guns. Once the turret gunner had the target in the cross hairs of his sight, he fired both guns simultaneously. A mechanism in the gun-sight accurately calculated the RADS deflection for the gunner. Not so for the flexible gunner. He only had one gun and had to make his own allowance for deflection measured in RADS, which was nothing more than a series of increments on the horizontal bar of his gun sight. He led the target with the maximum amount of RADS when his target was at nine o'clock or three o'clock. The only time he could fire directly at the target [in the cross hairs of his sight] was when the target was dead on. [At twelve, or six o'clock.]

There were four flexible guns on a B-17G. Two, on either side of the nose, were manned by the navigator when under attack. The last two were in the waist, one manned by the waist gunner, and the other manned by the radio operator when under attack.

Before my time, there was a flexible gun in the radio room manned by the radio operator. It was mounted in a Plexiglas bubble protruding from the top of the fuselage. This gun had been removed for two very good reasons. One being that too many radio operators shot up their own dorsal fins. [Turrets were electronically controlled to prevent this from happening.] The other was, that by having the radio operator man one of the waist guns if attacked by fighters, one waist gunner was eliminated, reducing the crew to nine men. This alleviated a serious manpower shortage, as well as reducing the overall weight of the aircraft, considering the man, his flak vest, helmet, gear, the gun, and ammunition. The fuel carried in the aircraft varied depending on the distance to the target. Lighter aircraft flew faster, higher, and consumed less fuel. Therefore, no more fuel was put in the aircraft than was necessary to safely complete the mission. A *maximum effort* required a full load of 2,780 gallons of fuel. We called a maximum effort, a *twenty-seven-eighty.*

Ground personnel spent all night refueling the planes being prepared for the upcoming mission, and the very first thing we wanted to know when we woke up in the morning was, *how much fuel was in those planes this morning.* And we found this out from the poor guy in the orderly room who had the job of waking us. He would open the door, switch on the lights, and as he walked through the barracks, he called out the numbers he knew we wanted to hear. If it was *twenty-seven-eighty,* he was greeted with moans, groans and curses; for we all knew that we were in for a very long and hard day.

7

~~~~~~

Sunday, January 21,
Mission number one: Aschaffenburg

THIS MORNINGS MESSAGE WAS NOT A TWENTY-SEVEN-EIGHTY. Although it was cold and damp out, I quickly dressed, rushed to the latrine, and shaved with cold water. There was no such thing as hot water for shaving or showering at Podington. Hot water required fuel, and fuel was a scarce commodity during the war. I felt that shaving was necessary though... even with cold water. In the next fourteen hours or more, at least six would be spent wearing an oxygen mask, and even *after* shaving that mask became miserable. Without shaving it was unadulterated torture.

Most everyone wanted a good breakfast, thirteen or fourteen hours was a long time between meals, so I then rushed to the combat mess hall. Combat crews enjoyed somewhat better food than noncombatants. Breakfast sometimes consisted of fresh eggs [cooked to order], fried potatoes, sausage or bacon, and toast with margarine and marmalade. Other times it was pancakes or French toast. And there was always lots of hot chicory flavored coffee. Breakfast was not always that good. On occasion, we were served powdered scrambled eggs.

These eggs were usually slightly green in color and tasted a little like sulphur. And then there was a dish we called SOS [and I don't think you want to know what that means]. It consisted of biscuits covered with a light brown gravy mixed with chipped or ground beef.

Shuttles waited outside while we ate. After breakfast they transported us to the briefing rooms, locker rooms, and then on out to our aircraft.

Now, for the first time, on January 21, I entered the long smoke-filled briefing room. The room was buzzing with conversation, sometimes punctuated by nervous laughter and an occasional cough. At the front of the room was a stage with a lectern. On the wall at the rear of the stage hung a large curtain.

I sat near the back of the room. Soon there was a commotion behind me, someone yelled *TEN-HUT*, and we all jumped to our feet and saluted. From the corner of my eye I saw our twenty-seven-year old Commanding Officer, Colonel James W. Wilson and his staff pass by in the now silent room.

"At ease, men," the Colonel said, as he passed. We all sat down. All eyes were on the group as they sat on a bench at the front of the room, obviously reserved for them . Colonel Wilson then nodded to the briefing officer as if to say, "Let the show begin." The officer stepped up to the lectern, shuffled some papers and cleared his throat.

"Good morning, gentlemen," he said. All eyes were now on the big curtain. The curtain was hiding a huge map of Europe showing our target for the day. The officer turned and pulled it open, disclosing the map. Sighs of relief enveloped the room. Two lengths of red twine were pinned to the map, one, representing the route into the target, and the other representing the route out. From the sighs, I gathered that the veterans did not consider this a really tough mission. The officer put the tip of his pointer on the spot we were interested in, where the two red lines converged on the eastern portion of the map.

"Your target for today," he said, "is Aschaffenburg." Aschaffenburg is in Bavaria, on the hilly banks of the river, Main. The officer swung his pointer to the western part of the map and put the tip on the red line.

"You will enter enemy territory here, at Egmond, on the coast of Holland," he continued. "You will pick up your fighter escort here, just south of the Zuider Zee. Then you will follow a course...."

As he talked, his pointer kept bouncing along the zigzagging red line, into and out of Germany. He gave us the location of our four check points, then discussed the latest intelligence reports regarding antiaircraft batteries and fighter opposition. At one time during the briefing he introduced the meteorologist, who gave us the latest weather forecast. Then the first officer fielded questions. You knew the briefing was about to conclude when he held up his stop watch and said...."Gentlemen, synchronize your watches. It will be 0530 in exactly fifteen seconds." I pulled out the stem of my Hack watch; set it for 0530, and waited for the count down, ". . . five... four... three... two... one... hack!" I pushed the stem in when he said "hack."

"Good luck Gentlemen," the man said, and the briefing was over.

⌘

As I made my way through the crowd I saw Tom Shanahan being blessed by his Chaplain. A Chaplain always waited near the door of the briefing room to serve men of their faith. At the door a communications officer passed out the day's code sheet to all radio operators. This sheet was necessary to encode and decode short wave radio messages. The code was changed every day.

In the locker room I noticed that some men carried their forty-five pistols in shoulder holsters. Mine was back at the barracks. I had elected not to carry it. Although I had done very well with other arms, my performance firing the forty-five left much to be desired. I also felt that I had a better chance of survival without it. It could give me a false sense of security and tempt me to 'shoot it out,' a foolhardy act I thought, since the forty-five pistol is by no means a match against German rifles or Lugers. Also, I heard, if you were lucky enough to hit your target you could count on one thing, your chances of living very long after that had greatly diminished.

I first donned my heated suit over my ODs. B-17s did not have pressurized heated cabins and temperatures would get as low as sixty degrees below zero. To keep warm, we wore electrically heated suits. The pants, jacket, slippers and gloves, all plugged into each other and then into a thermostatically controlled outlet in the aircraft.

Over the heated suit I wore a green gabardine one piece flying suit and a green fur collared flying jacket. Over my heated slippers I wore fleece lined leather flying boots. Next came a yellow inflatable vest called a 'Mae West,' named after a buxom vaudeville and movie star. The 'Mae West' kept you afloat and was fine in the summer, but was of little use in the North Sea or English Channel in the winter. Anyone in those waters in the winter would expire from exposure in minutes.

The vest saved you from drowning, but you would soon die of hypothermia.

Now I stepped into and carefully adjusted my parachute harness. A harness had to be very snug, so snug that you could barely straighten up. It was especially important that the straps straddled the scrotum. When a chute opens, the sudden impact is in the crotch and if things are not properly adjusted in that area, a man could forget about ever having descendants.

Using the shoelaces, I then tied street shoes to the left side of my harness at my hip. Many airmen were forced to surrender after bailing out simply because they had no shoes. The shock of the chute opening sometimes sent your boots flying, and even if they didn't, you couldn't walk far in flying boots, or slippers.

On that first mission I wore a white silk scarf, a gift from my mother, and would never fly a mission after that without it. It was my good luck charm. I put a small bible, another gift from my mother, in my left breast pocket. This bible, sitting on a shelf on my bookcase behind me as I write this, has a metal cover, on which is inscribed, *May God be With You.*

A story had been recently published in the U.S. newspapers about a bible like this. It supposedly stopped a piece of flak and saved an airman's life. The people making these bibles were now very wealthy, I thought. Every mother with a son in the service must have run out and bought one, just about everyone I knew had one.

Then I put my leather helmet on, snapped one side of my oxygen mask to the helmet and strapped a throat mike around my neck. As I shuffled off to the parachute room, an officer handed me an escape kit. Among other things, an escape kit contained a silk map of Europe [I still have one], high energy fudge, Benzedrine pills to keep you awake, and a small book of English translations of various foreign languages. The book contained phrases like *I need water.* Next to each phrase were translations, so by pointing to the English version, hopefully, the other party would understand. While most men were captured or killed, some successfully walked out of enemy territory. The escape kit went into a zippered pocket in the left leg of my flying suit.

In the parachute room I picked up a chest pack chute. I already had the harness on. We wore the harness at all times, but now I needed the proper chute that worked with that harness. Because of a shortage of American-made gear, we also used some British gear. If you had an American made harness on, you *had* to have an American-made chute [or vice versa]. As you already know, the British drive on the 'wrong' side of the street. And as you may have guessed, their chutes connect to the harness exactly opposite to ours. Built into the American harness, at your chest, were two snap type hooks. Two rings were built into the chute. If you had to bail out, you simply snapped the rings to the hooks and you were in business. But the British put the rings on the harness and the hooks on the chute. So if you were wearing a British harness and grabbed an American chute and had to bail out, you were SOL, if you know what that means. You would have rings on the harness and rings on the chute. The gear *was* color coded to help avoid this. Red stripes were sewn to the American gear. Yellow to the British.

Looking like an alien from another planet, I went outside and lumbered over to a shuttle. Before I boarded, I told the driver to let me off at aircraft one-four-four. Crews did not always fly the same aircraft. Early in the war they did, but not in my time. We had been informed earlier that Lapinski's crew would be flying aircraft

#144 [Actually #44-6144, however, we only went by the last three digits].

A Lt. Freeman would be our pilot today. Hank would be our copilot. Whitey was flying as copilot on another crew. It was a swop; SOP [Standard Operating Procedure]. An experienced pilot always flew with a crew on their first mission.

As the pilot, copilot and engineer started their preflight inspection, the rest of the crew picked up the guns at the gunnery shack adjacent to the hardstand and carried them to their respective positions on the aircraft.

When the preflight inspection was completed, the men up front entered the aircraft through the nose hatch. While the navigator and bombardier took up their positions in the nose, the pilot, copilot and engineer settled into the cockpit. The pilot in the left seat, the copilot in the right. The engineer stood behind them looking over their shoulders so he could observe the instruments. At the engineer's back was the top turret, the turret he would man if we were attacked by fighters. Behind the turret was the bulkhead separating the bomb bay from the cockpit. A door in the bulkhead opened out to the bomb bay.

A catwalk, about eight or ten inches wide, spanned the bomb bay leading to another bulkhead separating the radio room from the bomb bay. On each side of the catwalk were the bomb racks. Five-hundred pound bombs hung on the racks that day. There was just enough room between the bomb racks for a man to pass through to the radio room. Several feet below the catwalk were the bomb bay doors.

The wings, on both sides of the bomb bay, contained self-sealing fuel tanks. Coming from the bomb bay, the radio room door opened to your right. Immediately inside, to your right, was the radio operator's position.

He sat in a swivel bucket seat facing the nose of the aircraft. Immediately in front of him was a plywood writing shelf attached to the bomb bay bulkhead. Mounted on the shelf were a short wave radio receiver and a Morse code sending key. On the left side of the bucket seat was a Plexiglas window through which the radio operator could observe the left wing and the number one and two engines. Overhead, in the middle of the room, were two hatches. One, a removable Plexiglas escape hatch used by the crew to exit in the event of ditching. The other was no longer used. It was the hatch once used for the radio operator's flexible gun.

Looking toward the tail, another bulkhead and door separated the radio room from the waist. Fastened to this bulkhead, on the right-hand side of the door, was the radio operator's transmitting equipment. Just to the left of this door, was the IFF [Information Friend or Foe] equipment. This equipment automatically emitted a secret ultra high frequency radio signal that could only be detected by the British air defense network. In this manner they could differentiate between friendly aircraft, perhaps stragglers struggling home, and enemy aircraft hoping to sneak through the radar screen. For security reasons this apparatus was equipped with a self-destructing explosive. If the radio operator bailed out, his last duty was to pull the pin on this explosive as he passed the door on his way out. The apparatus blew up about fifteen seconds later.

On the other side of the radio room door, in the waist, was the top of the ball turret. The lower portion, with the guns, hung under the aircraft. The flexible waist guns were mounted in windows on each side of the waist. They were the responsibility of the waist gunner. When attacked by Bandits, the radio operator would come back and man the unattended gun.

There were four ammunition bins and belts in the waist, one feeding each gun. Looking toward the tail, the waist door was on the left. The tail gunner, when in his position, was hidden from view by the hydraulic shock serving the tail wheel. George, Les, Mal and I, entered the aircraft through the waist door. I went forward to the radio room and the others stayed in the waist.

For their safety during takeoff, ball turret and tail gunners were not allowed to take up their positions until the aircraft was airborne. It took a special kind of person to man these positions. I rode in both of them, but only once. The tail wasn't so bad, a little cramped and claustrophobic, but the ball turret was something else. You had to sit in a fetal position. I was five feet nine and weighed about one-hundred-forty pounds, and I barely got in there. The ball moved in any direction you pointed the guns. The view was fantastic, but when I swung that ball around every which way and realized that I was hanging underneath that plane in a Plexiglas ball, I couldn't get out of there fast enough. It was very scary. I always thought that the ball turret gunner had to be a little crazy, but was probably the most courageous man on the crew.

On the other hand, I thought that I had the best position of any man on the crew. Granted, I couldn't see as much as they could from the ball, nose, or cockpit, but sometimes that was a blessing. I had my own room, more freedom than the pilot, and a swivel bucket seat and desk. What more could a man ask for?

When flying missions I always latched the door to the waist in the open position so the waist gunner and I could keep an eye on each other. Next I checked to see if the ground-crew had delivered my box of chaff. Chaff, small bundles of tinsel, very similar to Christmas tree tinsel, was used to deceive enemy radar. It was the radio operator's duty to throw these bundles out a chaff chute starting at the IP [the initial point of the bomb run, about three to seven minutes prior to bombs away.]

Before reaching the IP the group could take evasive action to avoid antiaircraft fire, but, *on* the bomb run, they were dedicated to go straight to the target. There could be *no* evasive action once you were on the bomb run, *and the Germans knew it.* This is where they concentrated their fire power and this is when radio operators threw out their chaff. Chaff chutes were located on the fuselage in such a position that the radio operator could swing his bucket seat around facing the tail and throw the chaff out with his right hand.

Once in the bucket seat I stored my chute on top of the radio receiver. A radio operator could not perform his job with a chest pack chute in his way. I then plugged my heated suit, earphones and throat mike, into the electrical system and temporarily laid my flak vest and steel helmet under my seat. After entering the time and date in my log, I sat back and looked out the window on my left... the long nerve-racking wait now began.

Thirty-six aircraft would take off. Three squadrons of twelve planes each. There was a lead Squadron, High Squadron and Low Squadron. Each squadron consisted of three elements of four planes each; again, Lead, High, and Low.

The Group leader was the number one plane in his element, and he always took off first, followed by the Deputy Lead in the number two spot, then numbers three and four. Next, the High and Low elements of the group lead squadron took off in the same manner. The waiting time depended on three things. First, was the position in the group that your squadron was flying that day. Second, was the element you were flying in.

Third, and last, was the number you were flying in that element.

For example: if you were flying number four in the Low Element of the Low Squadron, you were the last plane to take off, commonly known as "Tail End Charley," the *second* most dangerous position in the group.

To cause confusion, and to take out our VIP, and one of our four elite crews in the group, German anti-aircraft gunners, and the Luftwaffe, went after our *Group Leader*. Making it the *most* dangerous position in a group.

"Tail End Charley's" happened to be the *easiest* aircraft for German fighters to pick off. To avoid detection, the German FW190s, in groups of four, would sometimes follow a group several thousand feet behind and above them. Then, the Luftwaffe's more maneuverable ME109s would engage our fighter escort in "dog fights."

The German pilots hoped... while we were all watching the spectacular "dog fights" instead of looking out for them, that their FW-190s could swoop down and take out our "Tail End Charley." This did not always work, but when it did, they could sometimes took out as many as two or three B-17s before the group knew it.

I don't know how long we waited that day, but it seemed like hours. As we had never taken off with a bomb load before, and this was my first mission, I was very apprehensive to say the least. At long last I saw the ground crew pulling the props through. B-

17s did not have automatic primers and each prop had to be manually turned ten times. Usually the aircrew performed this chore... when flying combat missions... the ground crew did.

First I heard the number one engine whine and cough. It sputtered and belched blue smoke. The sputtering turned to a mild vibration and the prop was now spinning smoothly. Soon number two did the same. I could only hear number three and four... there was no window on my right side.

In the cockpit, Freeman checked the hydraulic pressure, then waved to the ground crew-chief to remove the wheel chocks. With the chocks removed, he taxied from the hardstand to the perimeter strip. Braking, he asked Hank to unlock the tail wheel so he could turn onto the strip. Once on the strip, Hank locked the tail wheel again and we started the long taxi to the runway. Out my window I could see other aircraft belching blue smoke as we passed. When all thirty-six planes were in position along the perimeter strip, the squadron leaders called for an engine run-up.

"Brakes set," Hank said.

Freeman set the throttles at 1,500 RPM and the trim tabs at zero, then ran through the turbo and propeller exercises several times. Next he checked the generators. And while he watched the engine nacelles and cowlings for roughness, and Hank watched for any drop in RPM, he ran each engine up in turn.

On the interphone the squadron leader called each pilot to verify that they were ready to go. Then the group leader checked with the squadron leaders. It was almost "H" hour [take off time]. At the front of the line the leading element pulled out and turned, facing the long runway. At "H" hour the group leader started his takeoff. The number two man, the deputy lead, pulled up as soon as he saw the leader rolling. When the leader's wheels left the ground, the deputy lead started his takeoff. There was a thirty-second time lapse between takeoffs. As each plane took off, the next in line moved up and waited. Now, until the last two planes took off, there were always three planes on the runway, one taking off, the second halfway down the runway, and the third just starting to roll.

We kept moving up and stopping, moving up and stopping, until it was our turn. Freeman took it out on the runway and turned facing 5,000 feet of concrete. He set the brakes and pushed the throttles to full take off power. The sound of the engines was deafening, and the aircraft started to shake as if it were eager to go. One would think that once the pilot released the brakes, that Fort would literally *shoot* down the runway. But although we all grew to love this "big assed bird," as we sometimes called her, there was one thing about her we feared… she was always reluctant to leave the ground with a full load. And now, when Freeman released the brakes, she just seemed to waddle down the runway like a running goose.

While the engineer monitored the manifold pressure, RPMs and temperature gauges, Hank called out the air speed.

"Eighty… ninety… ninety-five…"

Ninety-five was the point of no return. Freeman was committed to take off now no matter what.

"One-hundred… one-hundred and five… ," Hank said.

Now Freeman had passed the stalling speed but we were still on the runway.

"One-hundred and ten… one-hundred and fifteen… one-hundred and twenty."

And that was it, the rumbling of the wheels stopped, we were off the ground but now had to clear the trees ahead. To reduce the wheel drag and increase air speed Freeman activated the landing gear motor to bring the wheels up. This was SOP and we heard it every time we took off, but today was different.

Pilot: "Wheels up!"

I heard the whine of the landing gear motor in the bomb bay.

Pilot: "Landing gear up left!"

Copilot: "Landing gear up right!"

Engineer: "Tail wheel up!"

Every fiber in my body seemed to stretch to the limit like rubber bands ready to snap. I saw the barren trees on the side of the runway merge as they flashed by in the blue grey dawn as we picked up speed. Then the engines *roared*... and we sailed out over the tree tops.

I breathed a sigh of relief and relaxed as the engines smoothed out and the trees fell away below. We were on our way to assembly and had passed the first deadly test. Safely in the air, traveling at 120 miles per hour, we were climbing at 400 feet per minute.

Although I never feared assemblies, they were extremely dangerous. There were many groups assembling in a close area. A split second error by one pilot could bring on a horrendous catastrophe. Midair collisions within a group, or with other groups, were not uncommon. Many planes and men were lost in this manner. However, it was not something you could see coming until it was too late.

This was our first assembly and I was awed by it. Though dangerous, they were always a sight to behold. We were in a crisp blue sky and bright morning sunlight now, even though dawn was just breaking below. We were so high now that contrails were forming. I watched as, one by one, each aircraft pulled into its assigned position around our squadron leader.

Leading the group today and making up the "point" of this modified "V" formation was the 407th. They had already assembled and were circling and climbing as the last squadron was still taking off.

Flying the low squadron and making up the left side of the formation was the 327th. They moved in lower and to the left of the lead squadron.

The 325th made up the high squadron and we moved into the right of, and higher than our group leader.

Back at the base the 326th was on standby. Once we were on our way to the target they would be dismissed. Most crews of that squadron would then be free for the rest of the day.

When all three squadrons were in formation, "Fame's Favored Few" struck a course in the direction of the frigid North Sea and the frozen Continent of Europe. We were still climbing and it was getting colder. I reached over and turned the thermostat for my heated suit up a couple of notches.

Mal was in the tail now, George was in the ball turret, and I could see Les scanning the skies and leaning against the right waist gun.

"Pilot to crew." Freeman broke the silence of the intercom. "We are at 10,000 feet now, time to go on oxygen."

It was SOP now for the pilot to call for an oxygen check at predetermined intervals. When the pilot called for an oxygen check, each man in turn would answer, starting with the tail.

"Tail OK."

"Waist OK."

"Radio OK," etc.

This procedure was necessary due to the dangers of anoxia, the Greek word meaning without oxygen, or oxygen want. Anoxia creeps up on the victim without him realizing it. It starts with a feeling of well being or exhilaration, similar to having too many alcoholic beverages. If the condition is not corrected, the victim will pass out and soon die. Several things could go wrong to cause this, an equipment failure, for example, or a leaky mask.

The U.S. Air Force suffered more casualties from anoxia and frostbite than from enemy action in World War II. In the case of frostbite many gunners lost fingers and even hands. Sometimes, if a gun jammed in the heat of battle, a gunner unwittingly took off his gloves and touched the sixty-degree below zero metal. His flesh would instantly stick to the metal and freeze.

Now began what would become the boring part of a mission… if anything about a mission could be called boring. A steady monotonous drone of the engines for hours upon hours. The silence of the intercom was rarely broken except for the pilot's oxygen checks.

The pure blue sky was now marred by miles of one hundred and forty-four contrails, one for every engine. As we climbed higher and higher I watched the English countryside below until the white breakers on the shoreline appeared, separating the land from the sea. And then, slowly, the land slipped away and was gone.

Over the North Sea, I was startled by the "pum-pum-pum" of the ball turret guns. I shouldn't have been startled but I was as nervous as a cat. When I realized that George Waldschmidt was only clearing [testing] his guns, I relaxed. Gunners were allowed to clear their guns over the English Channel or sea. However, it was not mandatory; George was one of the few gunners I flew with who did it religiously.

Soon the white shoreline of Holland appeared and I knew we were approaching enemy-occupied territory. [The Allies had bypassed the Netherlands due to the stubborn German resistance there.]As we crossed the shoreline and went deeper into the Netherlands, I was mesmerized. I was seeing the Continent for the first time and I knew there was a war going on down there. A war that I had seen so much about in newsreels, Life Magazine and movies. It was in all the newspapers and on the radio every day. People were busy killing each other down there, and it was, in most cases, perfectly legal. In fact they were getting paid for it. It was their job, and now mine too.

⌘

As I was flying over Holland for the first time on our way to the Zuider Zee, I was reminded of a picture I had seen recently of a young Dutch man and woman hanging by their necks from a lamp pole. They were Dutch Partisans, part of the underground fighting their Nazi occupiers. In all probability, I thought, I had relatives down there. My mother's father, Dennis Weiss, was born in Holland. He and his mother arrived in the States in the late 1890's when he was twelve years old. Shortly after they arrived, his mother died, making him an orphan. Consequently, he was raised and educated in a Catholic orphanage in New York.

As we flew over my grandfather's native land, I remembered a story Grandpa told me of how, when he worked on a freighter plying the Great Lakes in 1905, they threw ropes to Indians from the Walpole Island Reservation. They were chugging for Walleye Pike in the St. Clair River. The freighter would tow them from Algonac, all the way up to Port Huron, where the Indians would let go and chug all the way back to Algonac. The river has an eight mile per hour current. I caught a lot of Walleye's in that river myself, except I used an outboard motor.

Grandpa and I were very close. When I was in grade school I helped him out on his Indian Village bakery route during summer vacations. We plied his baked goods from a horse drawn wagon. His horse knew every stop on his route.

Back home in Michigan, I thought, Grandpa was still sleeping. So was the rest of my family. Their biggest problem when they wake up this morning will probably be if they have enough ration stamps to last the week.

⌘

Our 'Little friends' [P-51 Mustang fighter escort] interrupted my day dreaming when they pulled up out there beside us, over the Zuider Zee. They were out of range of course. We all knew, including our escort, that the German's had some Mustangs too. There were so many Mustangs out there, spread over such a large area, it would be easy for a German to slip in, then attack a Tail End Charley, say, and shoot one down before we knew it. So if a Mustang came in to close, even if he was waving an American flag and singing the Star-Spangled Banner, we would shoot him down. As much as we loved those guys, we took nothing for granted. So, besides constantly looking for Bandits... we had to keep an eye on the Mustangs too.

Later, as we neared the target, Bob broke the silence on the intercom, he said the IP was coming up in five minutes. Although I had a flak vest and helmet, this was the only mission I used them on. They were just too heavy and restricting. From that day on, I stored them under my bucket seat in the unlikely event that they would protect my backside. I then looked out the window. Our 'little friends' were peeling off and leaving us. No one in their right mind went in there if they didn't have to, and that included the Luftwaffe. Why get killed by your own flak? Better to go *around* the target and see who comes out of that mess. Of course, our 'little friends' did the same thing.

Leaving my seat, I opened the door to the bomb bay and latched it open, so I could see the bombs. It was my duty to tell the pilot if all the bombs were gone. Back in my seat I heard the whine of the bomb bay door motor and watched the doors open. My eyes smarted as the cold air blew in.

"Bomb bay doors open," Freeman said.

"Bomb bay doors open," I repeated.

This was SOP, I could see the doors were actually open; the pilot could not. Then I swung my bucket seat around and started throwing chaff out the chute, one bundle every two or three seconds. Each bundle was sucked out the chute and the tinsel was instantly scattered to the four winds. This worked so well at times tail gunners reported watching flak bursts following the tinsel down for thousands of feet. Unfortunately, there were times when we ran into very good radar batteries who were not easily fooled, and then there was hell to pay.

With my chaff gone, I swung back around and looked out the window. I heard a *WOOMPH* and felt the aircraft lurch. At the same instant four black puffs, each puff about the size of a five or six-foot circle, burst off our left wing. I had just been introduced to the German 88MM flak. Fixing my eyes on the bomb bay, I waited for those five hundred pound monsters to fall. I always felt better when they were gone.

"Bombs away," Ted said.

In the blink of an eye they tumbled down. The aircraft seemed to *leap* with joy with the release of that heavy load.

"Bombs away," I repeated.

When Freeman heard me repeat "bombs away," he knew they were all gone and he closed the doors. With the bomb bay doors up, I unlatched and closed the radio room door, then returned to my seat. The trip home that day was uneventful. Our 'little friends' left us somewhere over the Netherlands. We crossed the North Sea to the friendly shores of England, and flew inland to Podington.

As we circled the field at fifteen-hundred feet, the lead squadron peeled off and landed. Our squadron was next. When it was our turn to land, Freeman banked and leveled off. When he touched down I heard the familiar screech and bump. We hit again, this time more gently, and rolled to the end of the runway. Freeman turned and taxied down the perimeter strip to our hardstand. I watched as the crew chief directed him in. Then he turned the plane around facing the perimeter strip and cut the engines. We were home safe.

Waiting for the shuttle we were all smiles, although we had thirty-four to go, our first mission was under our belt, and we were still here to tell about it. Each crew was interrogated by S-2 [intelligence] separately. We sat around a table and answered the intelligence officers' questions. Free cigarettes and gum were available on the table. The officer took notes until he was satisfied that he had our version of what happened that day. Our first mission was fairly routine. There was not much to tell. But these sessions were much more important on missions when we suffered losses... were attacked by enemy fighters, or saw something unusual.

After the S-2 session, we went directly to the locker room, disrobed to our ODs, and caught the shuttle to the combat mess hall. Inside the door of the mess hall we paused at a table full of shot glasses filled with whisky. Every man on the mission that day was entitled to one glass. A medical officer stood by checking off our names.

Back at the barracks I removed a book and pen from my footlocker and sat on my bunk. The book, which I still have, is similar to a diary, its title is *LIFE IN THE SERVICE*. Under a section of that book called *Calendar of Events*, I then made the following entry:

Sunday, January 21, 1945.
Mission number one: Aschaffenburg.

[This narrative is based on notes I made in LIFE IN THE SERVICE, my memory, as well as others, my army records... and just about every letter I sent home... thanks to my father, God bless his soul.]

I am often asked, "What did you guys do when Mother Nature called?" Fortunately, there was only one thing I ever had to do, and for that we had a device called a 'relief tube.' This device consisted of a black plastic funnel hanging on a clip fastened to the bulkhead in the bomb bay, just behind the radio room.

You can believe me when I say, when flying missions at high altitudes, it was never easy to use this device. First you had to disconnect your throat mike, heated suit and oxygen mask, and then, if you were over ten thousand feet, connect your mask to a walk around bottle. With the walk around bottle under one arm, you went into the bomb bay, removed your glove from one hand, and while standing on the cat walk, you unzipped your one piece flying suit. Now remember, we were wearing a very snug parachute harness with a strap on each side of the place you had to unzip, which increased the level of difficulty. Once you accomplished this feat, you had to get through a heated suit, ODs and underwear. Then, because the temperature was about sixty degrees below zero, the body part you were after, having a mind of it's own, retreated as far as it could to avoid the cold. This took a lot of digging and gentle pulling to coax it out to do its job.

When you had managed this, you held the funnel as close as possible and started the relief part of the operation. The problem was… once this happened the plane usually lurched and everything would stop until you could get it going again. All this time you were hoping no one had used the device recently and the hose was not frozen.

The next day the weather took a turn for the worse, with snow, fog and ice. It was so bad that "Liberty" runs were canceled for days. A record low of seventeen degrees above zero was recorded at Podington on Saturday, January 27. But the weather man was predicting better conditions for the next day and our names were again on the alert list.

8

Sunday, January 28.
Mission number two: Cologne

MY DAY HAD BEEN GOING FINE SO FAR. That
is, until briefing. When I heard our human alarm
clock bark out the fuel load that morning, I thought we
could look forward to another 'milk run.' We had less
fuel on board than our first mission. But when the briefing
officer pulled the curtain and put his pointer on Cologne,
I heard a chorus of *"Oh shit!"*

Cologne was in what the old-timers called 'Happy
Valley.' Known to everyone else as the Ruhr Valley...
the major industrial center of Germany. It earned the
name 'Happy Valley' because of the intense and accurate
antiaircraft batteries protecting the area. In fact, it was
among the most heavily protected areas in Germany.
The men moaning and groaning in the briefing room
had been there before.

We were flying aircraft 144 again today, and Hank
was now in the left seat. Whitey in the right. On the IP,
I understood why the old timers were so upset. There
were acres of black flak out there. A thick carpet of
poke-a-dots and we were flying right through them.
Aschaffenburg had been a cake walk compared to this.

The concussions caused our aircraft to pitch and roll like a ship in a heavy sea. And now I heard a new sound, a pinging and clattering, as if someone was throwing pebbles at us. But it wasn't pebbles, it was shrapnel, and the shrapnel was going right through our aircraft leaving jagged holes of all sizes in our aluminum clad skin. Then I heard something completely unexpected, I couldn't believe my ears, Hank said we were going to do a *three-sixty.*

Moments before reaching the IP, the Group Lead pilot would trim his aircraft and set up his AFCE [Automatic Flight Control Equipment] under the direction of his bombardier. *At* the IP, and until *bombs away,* the bombardier actually took over the flight of the aircraft *through* the Norden Bombsight. During this time, the bombardier was in complete command. On occasion something would go wrong, and the bombardier knew he was irretrievably off the target. He would then call for a *three-sixty,* and the group would circle back and start the IP all over again. *Three-sixties* not only caused additional losses, they ate up precious fuel and forced many aircraft to abort before the day was over. And then there was the chaff. All the chaff was used up on the first bomb run. German anti-aircraft gunners loved three-sixties. Now they could rely 100% on their radar. Their guns were no longer shooting at phantoms. But… to justify *three-sixties…* if we could not hit our target, there was no use of our being there.

This was my first *three-sixty.* It would not be my last. Coming around on the IP the second time with no chaff, we really took a beating. An aircraft in the 407th blew up off our left wing. The giant turned into a big red and orange ball. Some pieces were hurtling toward earth four miles below, while others, like the wings and tail section, slowly fluttered down like leaves. As I watched, transfixed, they disappeared. I can't imagine *anyone* surviving that explosion, but I counted three chutes.

Shortly after *bombs away* we were out of it, and four hours later Hank cut the engines at the hardstand. As we waited for the shuttle, we counted the jagged holes in our Fort. When we left in the morning, we wanted a 'milk run,' no flak and no fighters. But once safely back at the hardstand, as long as no one was injured, we thought the more holes the better. It gave us something to brag about. When the shuttle got there that day, we had counted two-hundred and fifty holes, and we hadn't finished counting. It's a wonder no one was wounded or killed.

The guys that had to repair the aircraft were already crawling all over our ship as we drove away. They would patch up those holes and work all night on that plane and, hopefully, it would be ready to fly in the morning. S-2 confirmed our fears, only three chutes had been sighted over the target. The group had lost one aircraft and nine good men that day. So much for short missions. We had little time to mull it over though, our names were on the alert list and we would be off again in the morning.

Monday, January 29.
Mission number three: Koblenz

Our target for today was the city of Koblenz. The 325th would lead the group. This would be our third mission, and all in the same aircraft... 144. This was the same aircraft we had counted two-hundred and fifty holes in just yesterday. Remember, I said, *hopefully* it would be ready today. Evidently, the crew chief thought it *was* ready, but, while Hank was revving up the engines, he found something wrong. He reported the problem, and we were ordered to switch to another aircraft. That meant moving our guns to another hardstand and starting all over. As a result we were very late in taking off. The group was far ahead of us. Flying directly to the first check point we missed the group. We missed them again at the second. As we approached enemy territory it looked like we had no choice but to go in alone. Hank, not wanting to go in alone, tacked on to another group in the bomber stream. All I know about the group is that it had a black triangle and an 'L' on the tail.

Shortly after we joined the triangular 'L' formation, the two aircraft in front of us collided. I never saw the collision, my view was restricted to our left side. I could see nothing in front of us. It was all over in seconds. Someone up front yelled, then I saw a cloud of debris below us and it was all over. We went on and bombed with the 'L' group and completed the mission with no further incidents. Back over the U.K. we left the 'L' guys and returned to Podington. Tight formations were prone to accidents. Vapor trails [frozen exhaust from planes ahead] sometimes blinded pilots causing miscalculations. Then 'prop-wash,' [turbulence created by propellers], would sometimes bounce, or push one aircraft into another.

However, the advantages of tight formations outweighed the disadvantages. One advantage was that tight formations created a close concentration of bombs on the target. Another advantage was that it created a better concentration of fire power. There were 430 fifty-caliber machine guns in a formation of thirty-six B-17s. That was an awesome number of guns to face from the viewpoint of an enemy fighter pilot. German fighter pilots were brave, but not stupid. They looked for easy

A tight formation

targets, stragglers, cripples… and loose formations. With few exceptions, they were not Kamakazi pilots, their objective was simple: Shoot down as many bombers as possible without getting shot down yourself.

Thursday, February 1.
Mission number four: Ludwigshafen

I had played some darts last night and had consumed a few beers. This morning my head was aching, and if that wasn't bad enough it was so foggy we could barely find our way to the mess hall. How stupid this was, I thought, I could be back at the barracks sleeping. There's no way we'll get off the ground today. I would have bet money on it. But I had no choice but to follow the old adage, *Mine is not to reason why, mine is but to do or die.* So I sat there in the briefing room and listened. The officer was pointing to a place on the map where the Rhine River separates Manneheim and Ludwigshafen.

"Your target for today, gentlemen," he said, "is the rail and road bridge at Ludwigshafen, and you will be bombing today using PFF." PFF was a fairly new method of bombing developed in August of 1944. The system featured a new radar bomb sight allowing navigators to find targets even under conditions of zero visibility. It was officially known as H2X, but we called it 'Mickey.' I believe the 92nd only had one aircraft modified for H2X, and it was only used by group lead crews. These aircraft were called *Pathfinders*. The ball turret had been removed and replaced with radar equipment. Only navigators trained in H2X could use it. We called them 'Mickey Men'. They sat in the radio room across the aisle and on the right side of the radio operator.

[Although I didn't know it at the time, brother Glen was being trained in H2X at that very moment and would later become a 'Mickey Man' on B-29s. Besides flying thirty missions in B-17s in the ETO in WWII, he was destined to fly thirty-one missions in B-29s in Korea. A 20MM shell fired from a Chinese

MIG would explode in the radar room severing an artery in his left arm and would earn him the Purple Heart. It also left most of his left thumb numb.]

A meteorologist assured us the fog would be gone before we returned. Our Operations Officer assured us we would be able to take off. The first prediction was dead wrong. The second was only partly wrong. As we waited to take off... today in aircraft 288 [I never saw 144 again] I cradled my aching head in my arms on the desktop and dozed off. Suddenly I was awakened when the desktop slapped me in the face and my head literally bounced off it. I heard a *THUMP* and *KABOOM*. The tower was shooting off red flares and Hank killed the engines.

George, Mal and Les, had been standing in the waist, and now with the engines cut, they went out the waist door to see what was going on. I followed. We gathered under the nose on the wet concrete, but the fog was so thick all we saw up ahead was the tail of the next aircraft. We knew that something dreadful had happened but it was just like a traffic jam on the expressway, we heard the sirens but we could see nothing. Soon word was passed back that one of our planes had crashed at the end of the runway, one of our worst nightmares. We had all heard the story about a plane stopping at the end of the runway last year in a fog like this. They say that the pilot turned around and started to taxi back up the runway only to be hit head on by the plane taking off behind him. I still can't figure that one out. As you can imagine, that made an awful mess. Heads, arms, legs and other body parts were found all over the place when the fog lifted. But that didn't stop 'Fame's Favored Few.' We did what they said they did last year, we were simply diverted to another runway. The only trouble was, the runway we were diverted to was shorter than the one we were on. That was certainly scary. One of our planes never made it on the *long* runway, now we were going to try one of the *short* runways. But before the morning was over, thirty-five planes had assembled over the fog and we were on our way to the continent.

It was on February 1, 1945 that I first became disenchanted with weather forecasters. When we arrived back at Podington, the fog was just as bad as when we left. This was not what they had predicted. There were no instruments for landing in fog in those days. Missions were normally canceled if fog was expected on our return. But the fog was not expected, so that day, to help the pilots, they started a fire on the far end of the runway and shot up flares. The fire and flares were supposed to help the pilots land, but all Hank could see in the distance was a red glow. He really couldn't see the runway until our wheels were about to hit. It was then that he discovered that we were off track. We were at a cross angle and about to hit a field of mud. Someone in the nose yelled, *"Pull 'er up!"*... of course, Hank saw it too, and about a fraction of a second before our wheels hit the mud all four engines roared and we started back up into the fog. Hank had no choice now but to climb back out of that fog, wait until everyone else landed, and try again. *Only now we were climbing blindly up through the rest of the group coming in to land.* The other guys must have been as scared as we were, they knew what was happening because they were listening to the tower, but we could do nothing but keep our fingers crossed and pray. Just as we came out of the clouds one of the crew yelled *"Plane!"* Hank pulled her back so hard I thought the wings flapped. I was pinned to my seat. It was so close I swear I could see the terrified eyes of the other pilot as we zoomed past him into the clear blue sky above. My pulse slowly returned to normal as we circled in silence and waited for the last plane to land. On his second attempt Hank hit the runway at the correct angle and we landed safely. When I jumped to the hardstand, my knees were shaking. As for the accident on takeoff... no one survived. That 'milk run' cost us one aircraft and nine good men.

9

Saturday, February 3.
Mission number five: Berlin

WE WERE IN A SPIN. I was pinned to my seat and couldn't move. I couldn't lift a hand to reach my chute sitting right there in front of me on my receiver. Then, suddenly I was in midair with no chute, the plane had broken up. I had seen other planes break up like this, but now it was happening to me. I was falling and falling, The ground was getting closer, I knew I was about to die!

Just then the barracks door slammed and I woke in a sweat. My heart was pounding and my chest was heaving. Only one guy would dare let the door slam like that at this time of the morning, and that would be the orderly. Normally I would resent his intrusion, but this morning I welcomed it. I heard the click of the light switch, then footsteps walking down the aisle. My heartbeat was slowing but I feared the worst… and I was not disappointed.

"TWENTY-SEVEN-EIGHTY!" he shouted. And there it was… he'd said the three words we never wanted to

hear. Our fifth mission would be our first *twenty-seven-eighty!*

It's funny how difficult it is to remember some things that happened so long ago, while others you never forget. February 3, 1945 was more than a half century ago, but it is a day permanently etched in my mind. I have since discussed this mission with George Waldschmidt in 1960, at his home in Fort Wayne, Indiana, and Hank Lapinski, as recently as 1995 at my home in Florida. We all agreed on the major details I am about to relate.

It started with that horrible dream. I had heard of a similar incident told to me by the man it actually happened to, my barracks-mate, Mel. It happened on January 8, when Mel bailed out over France. Only he had been lucky enough to put his chute on *before* he was pinned to his seat. Once pinned, he said, he couldn't move, not even a finger. It felt like he weighed tons. Then he blacked out. But he came-to in midair. The plane had broken up and he had been thrown clear. He simply pulled his rip cord, the chute popped open, and he landed safely.

February 3, had been picked by the Allies as the day to carry out a long planned operation called *Thunderclap.* This plan was devised to deliver one mighty death blow to a large German city by creating a 'fire storm' using the combined Air Forces of Britain and the United

States. It was conceived to break the morale of the German people.

The stars were shining brightly on that crisp clear morning as I entered the briefing room. From the moment I sat down, like everyone else, I never took my eyes off that big white curtain. Like all *twenty-seven-eighties* I experienced afterward, you could hear a pin drop as the officer reached over and pulled the cord exposing the huge map. Groans and "Oh shits" erupted from the guys up front, they could see the target, I could not. But I *could* see the zigzagging red lines converge deep inside Germany. The briefing officer slowly scanned the audience and patiently waiting for silence.

"Good morning, Gentlemen," he said. "Today you will participate in the greatest daylight raid the world has ever seen, and your target will be, *Berlin!*"

Accounts of the events of Saturday, February 3, 1945 will tell you that Marshall Zukov's armies were approaching the Oder River. Berlin was jammed with refugees fleeing the Soviets, and before this day was over more than 1,000 heavy bombers from the 8th Air Force would drop thousands of tons of bombs on that city.

I sat through the rest of that briefing slowly growing numb. My dream last night surely didn't help, and now I recalled other stories I had heard of the 'Big B' [*Berlin*]. These stories always included oceans of flak and enemy fighters as thick as flies in a barn. This wasn't the first time the 8th was going to Berlin, brother Glen had been there only months ago. What made this day different was the size of the raid.

All but paralyzed with fear, I got up and went about making preparations for the mission as if I were in a trance. If I could have thought of an honorable way to get out of that mission, I believe I would have. I *could* feign sickness. But who would believe me? Flying *was* voluntary. I could go to the flight surgeon. But I'd be branded a coward and sent home. Then how could I live with myself. Then, before I knew it, it was too late, I was on the shuttle and dropped off at the hardstand of aircraft #479. I don't remember her name, but I'll call her 'Little Miss.'

We did all the preflight stuff and soon Hank was revving up the engines. There was no getting out of it now. I just sat at my desk, logged in, and tried to resign myself to the fact that I wasn't coming back from this one. In other words, I was a dead man walking.

[I didn't know it at the time, but I wasn't the only one with such thoughts. Most men flew combat with some degree of fear. The important thing was… how they handled that fear.]

Our route as briefed would take advantage of water. We would cross the North Sea, fly over the East Frisian Islands and enter Germany somewhere near Bremerhaven. Taking a southeasterly course, we would pass over Lower Saxony. Crossing the Elbe near Burg we would turn due east somewhere near Beeskow, then swing northwest and start our bomb run. Taking advantage of a tail wind we would hit our target and continue northwest all the way to the North Sea, somewhere east of Hamburg. Over the North Sea we would turn and head directly for home.

The weather was perfect, not a cloud in the sky. Long before we reached the IP other groups were passing us on their way home. My friends in the nose, and George in the ball turret, always saw most things long before I did because of their magnificent view. And today their exclamations tipped me off to the dangers that lie ahead. Exclamations like,

"JEE-ZUS CHRIST! LOOK AT THAT FLAK!" and *"HOLY-SHIT!"*

I looked out my window and saw a carpet of black flak. It looked as if you could walk on it. We were now on the IP. I swung my bucket seat around and threw out the chaff. When the chaff was gone I swung back and stared into the bomb bay waiting for Hank to open the doors. More *WOOMPHS* vibrated through 'Little Miss,' then I saw daylight as the doors slowly opened. I heard the intercom click on and Hank said, "Bomb bay doors open." That meant he threw the switch, but he couldn't see if they were open or not. It was my job to repeat, "Bomb bay doors open." Then the bombardier knew they were open and he could release the bombs when ready.

On this mission only, I then did a strange and stupid thing, following an irresistible impulse, I knelt at the open bomb bay door and looked down at Berlin, more than four miles below. The wind made my eyes burn but I was fascinated by the sight. Almost half of the city was obscured by white smoke. A rim of fire, stretching for miles, was spreading over the city. Hundreds of red flashes [exploding bombs from the groups up ahead] were going off everywhere.

As Fossberg threw his toggle switches, he said "Bombs away!" I watched as they fell to make sure none hung up. Then I repeated "Bombs away." When Hank heard me, he knew they were all gone, and he could close the doors. I heard a *WOOMPH* nearby and quickly closed my door to the bomb bay and returned to my seat.

We heard *WOOMPH S* all around us now and 'Little Miss' was pitching and rolling. I heard a *WHACK* and saw sawdust floating around the room. I had been gripping the plywood desktop with both hands and had felt a sharp vibration, I looked down, and there, directly in front of me, was a jagged hole in the plywood. A piece of shrapnel had entered the floor between my legs, gone clean through the shelf and left a hole in the Alclad ceiling.

Then a loud *WOOMPH* just below us made 'Little Miss' jump and all hell broke loose. Everything happened so fast. I remember someone in the cockpit yelling, *"Number four's running away! HANK! FEATHER NUMBER FOUR!"*

The guys in the nose must have lost their oxygen supply because someone up front was calling for 'walk around bottles.'

The ball turret motor whined behind me and as I turned to look, George leaped out so fast he fell flat on his face. His oxygen had gone too. As George scrambled to hook his mask to the spare position in the waist, Les was jumping around on one foot screaming that he'd been hit. I had been trained in first aid back at Scott Field and was the official first aid man on the crew. As I prepared to go to the waist, George waved me off. He had taken a quick look at the waist gunners leg and found that Les had only suffered a bruise.

Now I looked at *my* oxygen gauge and saw the needle slowly moving to the red zone, I knew then that *I too*. . .would soon be out of oxygen.

We were losing altitude fast, almost in a dive as the cockpit finally feathered number four. They continued to take her down until we were under ten thousand feet, then they leveled off. As we were going down, I craned my neck and watched our group get smaller and smaller as we fell away. I never will forget the forlorn feeling of watching our group turn into tiny specs almost two miles above us, and realized that we were all alone over the center of Berlin with no 'Little friends' to protect us.

We took off our masks and George returned to his turret. Hank called the leader, described our circumstances, and asked for fighter cover.

"Roger, Wilco, Good luck. Over and out," our leader said.

The fact that we were alone, a crippled sitting duck, and still over Berlin, was frightening. From all the stories I had heard I expected German fighters would be swarming all over us any second now. Then an alarming exchange took place over the intercom. It went something like this:

Hank: "Pilot to navigator, give me a heading."

Bob: "I don't know where we are Hank, but I'm working on it."

Hank: "What the hell do you mean you don't know where we are!" *De-ja-vu* all over again, I thought.

Bob: "See that group up there at eight o'clock? Follow them until I get a bearing, they're going to England."

The group Bob was talking about was high above us and several miles west. They were also going faster than we were, they had four engines. Nevertheless, they *were* going toward the Baltic Sea.

[Years later, when discussing this mission with my brother, the navigator, Glen rightfully, came to Bob's defense. He said that, with all the things going on around him for at least ten or fifteen minutes, there

*was no way Bob could have given Hank a heading at
that particular time.*]

As we now limped over the suburbs just outside
of the German Capitol, all gunners were constantly
scanning the skies for fighters, *preferably ours.* The
group we were following soon disappeared. Still no
escort. Then Ted came on the intercom from the nose. It
sounded like he was talking to Bob.

"Is that what I think it is at 11 o'clock? Looks like a
hell of a lot of flak!"

"That's got to be *Hamburg,* Bob seemed to mutter.
Then, much louder, and with more conviction, he
said "That group we're following *must* be bombing
HAMBURG!" Then he soon came up with a heading,
around Hamburg, not over it.

As we approached the Baltic Sea alone, Hank asked
George Waldschmidt if he could see any fuel leaking.
I heard George swing the ball turret around, then he
answered in the negative. A few minutes later Hank
addressed the crew on the intercom and evaluated our
circumstances.

"Our number four engine's been feathered," he said,
"and we've lost the power in number two. That means
we only have two engines left… numbers one and three.
We've taken several fuel readings and the results are so
inconsistent there's no way of telling how much fuel we
have left. Something must be wrong with the gauges.
And because George did not see a leak, did not mean
there were no leaks. Small leaks could vaporize and be
difficult to detect. Following our route as briefed will
take us back over the Baltic and North Sea. There's
no way we can do that now," he said. "There's a real
possibility that we may have to ditch, and in that case
I want to be as close to land as possible. No one can

survive in these waters for long in a dingy." Concluding, he said, "We have two choices, we can go to Malmo, Sweden, or we can try and make it back to the base. And it doesn't look like we're going to get any fighter support." He was very democratic. He called for a vote. Sweden or Podington? Starting with the tail.

As I saw it we still had at least four hours of flying time to go, and most of it was over enemy territory, and then there was the 'Big Ditch' [English Channel] to cross. We had been on our own for almost an hour now with no sign of an escort. If the Germans didn't get us, the elements would. Certainly we could not be criticized for going to Sweden. And since I had heard stories of how the beautiful blond Swedish women loved American fliers, Sweden was much more appealing to me than doing this again, so I voted for Sweden. But was I shocked, and disappointed, the majority voted for England!

Hank then dropped 'Little Miss' down so that we were just above the trees. We were less likely to be detected that way. It was very beautiful country, lots of snow, pines and rugged hills. Eventually the terrain smoothed out and we neared the North Sea. Over the North Sea, Hank turned south, hugging the shoreline in case we had to ditch. We passed the shores of the East, and then the West Frisian Islands. Then we continued south along the coast of occupied Holland to Belgium. As we flew along the Belgium coast, Hank came on the intercom and addressed the crew. He said he was going to try and make it over the Channel, but if we couldn't, we should be prepared to ditch.

Then, as he turned out over the 'Big Ditch,' he told me to send a QDM to the British Air Sea Rescue Network asking the network to stand by for an SOS. I tuned my transmitter to the correct CW frequency,

and in Morse code sent a message to the British
Air Sea Rescue network. I identified myself, then
requested a QDM. They should have acknowledged
me but I heard no response. Nothing but static. Double
checking everything, I tried again. Still nothing but
static. Something must be wrong with my transmitter,
I thought. It must have been hit by shrapnel. The plane
was full of holes. But I decided to try it anyway, just in
case.

After I clicked out the message, I held my key down
for one minute, just like I did in Texas. If they heard
me, the Network would shoot a 'fix' on my signal. If
this procedure went according to plan, a network of
three radio stations along the coast of England would
determine our location. They would draw lines on
a map originating one line from each station in the
direction they received my signal. Our exact position
could then be determined at the point where these three
lines converged. Each time I repeated the procedure,
they could plot a new position. Then, by measuring
the distance we had traveled from the last position and
figuring the time between fixes, they could calculate our
air speed *and* heading. With this information they could
anticipate our location at any given time. If we were
to actually ditch, I would clamp my key down sending
them a continuous signal until the radio went dead.
Some crews ditched and were picked up within minutes
using this procedure, however, many *more* expired
waiting.

In between sending my messages I mentally went
over my role in the ditching procedure. The crew, with
the exception of the pilot and copilot, would gather in
the radio room. After I clamped my key down, I would
wait for the pilot's ditching message. Twenty seconds
before we hit the water the pilot was supposed to tell me

to brace for ditching. Then I would repeat this message to the crew and we would assume the ditching position; sitting with our backs to the bulkhead, facing the rear of the plane, with our heads between our legs.

We could expect two impacts. The first, a mild jolt when the tail struck the water. The second, a severe shock when the nose struck. Immediately after impact the pilot and copilot would exit onto the wings through the cockpit windows.

It was my duty then to remove the Plexiglas window in the overhead hatch and drop to my hands and knees. One by one the crew would step on my back and go out the hatch joining the pilot and copilot on the wing. I would then be the only man left in the plane. After I handed the pilot various emergency equipment, including a radio called the Gibson Girl, he would reach in and pull me out.

⌘

A very popular song of the time went, *There'll be blue birds over, the White Cliffs of Dover, tomorrow, just you wait and see.* I knew that song by heart, and the first land we sighted crossing the Channel as we struggled home that day were those beautiful white cliffs.

As we passed over those cliffs I thought, *On this day, at least one bird flew over the White Cliffs of Dover, and it was our Little Miss.*

As we approached the runway at Podington we thought we must be running on fumes. We had the runway all to ourselves and Hank went right on in. Our big tires screeched as 'Little Miss' touched down. She rolled to the end of the runway and stopped. Hank turned and started to taxi toward the perimeter strip. But he never made it. The last two engines sputtered and stopped, and there was dead silence. We had run out of gas.

I watched out the window as an elated ground crew raced toward us in a jeep waving and cheering. They were followed by a cleat track. They quickly hooked 'Little Miss' to the cleat track and pulled the battered aircraft to its hardstand. As we jumped to the concrete we were met by broad grins, firm handshakes and lots of hugs.

Most everyone else had given up on us, but not the ground-crew, they were always the last to give up on *their* ship, and the men who flew her. I will never forget that moment and those men. There was a lump in my throat, and from that day on, I bonded with ground-crews. God love them.

Two jeeps picked us up and drove us in. As we left the line, another ground-crew, still waiting, waved to us as we went by. They waited in vain though. Lt. Morrow, of the 325th, was last seen going down in flames over the 'Big B.' No chutes were sighted.

It was dark when we arrived at the all but abandoned S-2. Our story was recorded and we were crossed off the MIA list. At the practically empty combat mess, I gratefully accepted the extra whiskey ration offered to me by Whitey, a teetotaler.

Back at the barracks I had no sooner flopped on my bunk and I heard static on the 'squawk box' [two way communications system between the barracks and orderly room].

"Sergeant Thornton," a voice said.

"Ho!" I said from my bunk.

"The Communications Officer wants to see you ASAP."

As I slipped into my flight jacket and put on my cap, I wondered, *What the hell does he want me for?* This request was highly unusual.

My bicycle had been stolen recently so I had to make the long walk to the line in the dark. It was cold and just as I got there it started to drizzle. When I entered the captain's office, I came to attention and saluted.

"Sergeant Thornton reporting Sir!" I said. The room was dark except for a green shaded desk lamp. I could see the captain was holding *my* log under the light.

"At ease." He said, without looking up. When he apparently had finished with my log, he looked up and asked, "Sergeant, do you know how much it costs us in Lend Lease when the British Air Sea Rescue goes out after one of our aircraft?"

"No sir," I said. I knew very little about Lend Lease. It was not one of the subjects covered in our indoctrination or training. The Captain mentioned some astronomical sum and continued. "Do you know they've been out there looking for you 'till we just called them off when you came in? Why didn't you cancel your stand by on SOS? They thought you went down!"

I was about ready to drop from fatigue. A couple of hours ago I had grave doubts about ever seeing this base again. My hair was plastered to my head from wearing a leather helmet all day and except for the clean white area that had been covered by my oxygen mask, my face was all grime. On top of that, my practically new flying suit had slits up the leg, cut by the piece of shrapnel that had gone clean through the radio room, missing my head by inches. Someone had stolen my bicycle and it just started to rain. This had been a *very* bad day.

"As you can see by my log sir, they never acknowledged my transmission. I assumed that my transmitter had been damaged and they never received my message."

"Yes, I see that sergeant, and I saw your aircraft, you're very lucky. Obviously there's nothing wrong with your transmitter, but there must be something wrong with your receiver." He closed my log and said, "I'll have it checked out." Then, smiling, he said, "Welcome back soldier, get some sleep, you look like you need it." I saluted and left the room. From that day on, however, I had a genuine respect for the British Air Sea Rescue.

[In 1995 I felt better about this when Hank Lapinski, in my kitchen in Florida, read this and said, "You got off easy, Colonel Wilson really chewed my ass out for not canceling that message… it wasn't your fault, I should have given you the order to cancel it."]

Now I had to walk back to the barracks in the mud and rain. I hadn't gone very far when the brakes of a Jeep squeaked as it stopped beside me.

The Jeep had blackout covers on the lights.[Leaving a narrow horizontal slit for an opening.] It was enclosed, but the door was open and a voice came out of the dark asking, "Want a ride soldier?" I gladly hopped in the back seat and said "Thanks." It was very dark in there as I looked at the passenger beside me. Then I thought I was in *real* trouble, my good Samaritan was Colonel Wilson, and I had *not* saluted. But he said nothing about that, instead he seemed more interested in what happened to us over Berlin. He never mentioned my message. Although I had not flown with him yet, somehow I felt that he knew who I was and why I was walking in the rain.

Back at the barracks, I warmed my backside while I dried off by the stove and told my barracks mates what happened. All the men in my barracks had returned safely, but we all knew that our squadron had lost nine men that day, something we never talked about.

10

AS IT TURNED OUT, THE FIRST ATTEMPT AT *THUNDERCLAP* HAD FAILED. Berlin was still there and the Germans had not given up. But the mission was our fifth and our crew became recipients of the Air Medal. The engineer and I were promoted to Staff Sergeant and the gunners were promoted to Sergeant. And if that wasn't enough they threw in a three-day pass. Our first.

I don't remember what the others did on that three-day pass, but Mal and I decided to see London, a short train ride from Wellingborough. In London we took our first ride in an English taxi and checked into the Regency Palace on Piccadilly Circus, I still have the hotel receipt. Not being familiar with English currency yet, we just gave the cabdriver a five-pound note and hoped he would give us the right change.

The very first thing we wanted was a hot bath. Having not had the pleasure of hot water since we left Gander. Immediately, we learned something new about the British culture. Although the Regency was considered a good hotel in those days there was no private bath in our room. There were two very nice bathrooms on each floor. One at each end of the hall. In order to use the facility for whatever reason, it had to be unoccupied. And sometimes that could be a long wait if someone was bathing and shaving, etc.

But we managed, then dressed in our best ODs, a clean shirt, tie, sharply creased pants and brown spit and polish shoes. We also wore a new Eisenhower jacket sporting the 8th Air Force patch on the left shoulder and our new rank on our sleeves. Polished silver wings were pinned over our left breast pocket. On our right breast, we displayed our Air Medal, Battle of the Bulge, European Theater and Good Conduct ribbons. After a last minute look in the mirror we put on our hat with the Air Force insignia pinned over the visor, cocked it, donned our overcoats and proudly walked through the lobby onto the street, ready to explore the big city.

Although the city was in a blackout, we managed to satisfy our appetites at a fine restaurant, then moved on to a first class pub. Wailing air raid sirens distracted us as we eyed the ladies and sipped warm draft Mild or Bitters. Mal looked at me and asked, "What now?"

"When in Rome do as the Romans do," I said. I expected the patrons to proceed to the nearest shelter and we would follow. But they ignored the sirens and continued with their drinking and conversations as if nothing were happening. Glasses behind the bar jingled with the occasional thump and rumble of the bombs, but we appeared to be the only people in the place that noticed.

Since this was our first experience on the other end of an air raid, we decided to venture outside and see what it looked like. Because of the blackout, it had been completely dark when we arrived, but now there were hundreds of searchlights scanning the sky. Instead of the antiaircraft making black puffs, as we knew them, they made red flashes in the night and sounded like the finale of a 4th of July fire works program. A red glow of burning buildings rimmed the horizon. Ambulance and fire truck sirens mingled in all the confusion. We heard a few thumps and rumbles and returned to the bar.

"Ya know Yank, ya shouldn't ah done that, you can get yourself killed do'in that," the bartender said. This experience made it a little easier on my conscience as I later watched our bombs tumbling out of the bomb bay headed for Germany below.

I later learned that what we had observed that night was an attack of V-1s, the first unmanned jet, and the first of the German's 'vengeance weapons.' They called them, 'Flying Bombs,' the British called them 'Doodle Bugs,'and we called them 'Buzz Bombs.'

The V-1 was manufactured by Volkswagen. It traveled at 400 MPH and carried an eighteen-hundred-fifty pound warhead. The warhead went off after the V-1 ran out of fuel and dove to the ground. You were all right as long as you could hear the put-put of the engine, but if it stopped, you hit the ground and prayed. More than nine thousand V1s were launched by the Germans during the war.

[The V-2 was the second generation of German V weapons. It was a liquid fueled rocket masterminded by Dr. Werner Von Braun, the same man who later became the father of the American space program. Dr. Von Braun developed the rocket at Peenemunde under the direction of Colonel Walter Dornberger.
It was also the first of its kind. Unmanned, it delivered a one ton warhead without warning. Before falling, it reached heights of as much as fifty miles above the earth. Both V weapons were devised to terrorize populations, they had no guidance devices or military objectives. Their only purpose was to kill civilians.]

On our return to Podington we were saddened to find another empty bunk in our barracks. Engineer George Cook was killed by a burst of flak over Lutzkendorf.

Bad weather prevailed for the next few days and we were 'stood down.' However, on February 13, the weather improved and we were on the Alert List to fly the next morning.

11

Ash Wednesday, February 14.
Mission number six: Dresden

"YOUR TARGET FOR TODAY," THE BRIEFING OFFICER SAID, AS HE PUT HIS POINTER AT THE END OF THE TWO RED LINES, "IS THE NEWSTADT [NEW TOWN] RAILROAD STATION IN DRESDEN." I had never heard of Dresden, but I knew one thing before I arrived at the briefing room, this was to be another *twenty-seven-eighty!* And that fact alone gave me the jitters. This target was further east than the 'Big B.' In fact, by rail it is 111 miles southeast of the Capital, and not far from the border of Czechoslovakia.

"You will be following up on two strikes made last night by the RAF," the Briefing Officer continued, "Russian troops are only seventy miles from the city. Our objective is to disrupt transportation to the eastern front." I assumed by this statement that this strike was supposed to help the Russians.

"You will enter enemy territory here, at Egmond, on the coast of Holland," and he rested his pointer on Egmond. His pointer then jumped further along the red line. "You will pick up your fighter escort here, just south of the Zuider Zee." It seemed to me I'd heard all this before.

"You will follow a course almost due east to Quackenbruck." The pointer continued to jump along the red line. "There you will turn southeast and follow a straight line to Waltershausen. Here you turn northeast to Torgau and follow the Elbe to Dresden."

[The two air strikes carried out by the RAF on the night of February 13, 1945, followed by two consecutive days of bombing by the 8th Air Force, have become the most controversial air strikes ever performed by the Allies in the ETO. These raids sent shock waves around the world and the controversy goes on to this day.

I knew little about the politics of the mission until 1963 when I first read John Irving's book "The Destruction of Dresden." My reaction to the book was a defensive one. I thought the book had to be biased. So I set out to learn more about the subject. I then found it mentioned in John Toland's Pulitzer prize winning book "The Last 100 Days." It appeared again in 1969 in "Slaughter-House Five," by Kurt Vonnegut Jr., who said he was an eyewitness to the tragedy. Evidently he was an American POW billeted in an empty slaughter house in Dresden those fateful days. Then, in 1984, I read "Dresden 1945: The Devils Tinderbox," by Alexander McKee.

With the exception of "The Last 100 Days," I believe these books condemned the raids. Little, if anything, is said of the many atrocities committed by the Germans long before the Americans entered the war. Many Americans thought that Dresden had very little military significance. It was called "the Florence on the Elbe" and was known the world over for its historical architecture and art treasures.

But so was Coventry, in England, yet the Germans destroyed it in 1940, five years earlier.

It is probably true that on February 13, Dresden was swollen to twice its size with refugees fleeing the advancing Russians. It is also probably true that, as described in these books, the raid of more than 700 British Lancasters that night created a howling whirlwind of incineration the likes of which the civilized world had never seen before. And that this attack was followed by 300 B-17s striking on the 14th. Then another 200 on Thursday, February 15.

But, it is also true that more than six million Jews perished in Nazi concentration camps. And they knew for days, weeks and months, that they were going to die, and how they were going to die. They even knew beforehand that the Nazis were going to take all of their assets, even the gold in their teeth.

Also, in an undeclared war, during the Blitzkrieg, much of Warsaw, Rotterdam, London and Coventry were destroyed, just to name a few. And, as I mentioned before, V1s and V2s had <u>NO</u> military targets, and were not just aimed at the U.K., they also landed in Belgium, France, and the Netherlands.

I would also remind people of the Nazi's unscientific medical experiments on prisoners, and that these prisoners died a slow excruciating death. After studying all of these atrocities and more, I have no guilty conscience for participating in the Dresden raid. I only believe that it was unfortunate that the plan didn't work. Had it worked, many Allied soldiers, as well as Germans, would have lived to a ripe old age. Our Air Force should apologize to no one for these raids. The German people could have, and should have, ended that war long before it came to a "Dresden."]

As on all missions, I threw my chute into the bed of the personnel carrier and hoisted myself over the tailgate, then told the driver to drop me off at the aircraft we were flying that day, #677. When the shuttle stopped and the driver called out '*six-seven-seven*' I jumped onto the hardstand with my chute tucked under my left arm. Then my heart sank. Sitting there in front of me had to be one of the oldest planes on the base. It had a dull brownish green camouflage surface, not the sleek silver aluminum of the newer planes. They quit the practice of painting the planes some time ago, since this surface created a certain amount of drag, and was less fuel efficient. The only silver on this old timer was the hundreds of patches that made her look like on old quilt. I wondered how many missions she'd been on. My only consolation was that she was still here... not scattered all over the German countryside.

On the other side of the coin, one wondered how an aircraft like this could handle the stress of the wings flapping when trying to pull out of a dive.

Anyway, she got us off the ground and all the way to the target. Flak over the city was intense. We were on the IP and I waited to hear "Bombs away." Instead, I heard that we were going to do another *three-sixty.* As always on *three-sixty's,* there was no chaff left for another run. So when it came to using chaff to throw off the German radar, we were SOL.

When the group came around again, smoke trailed the number four engine of an aircraft in the 407th. Its prop slowed and stopped. Then the unfortunate aircraft peeled off and started down fast. In a few moments it was gone. I saw no chutes. After releasing our bomb load on the MPI we started our long trip home. Three crews were forced to land on the Continent to refuel that day, and the aircraft in the 407th, the one that disappeared over the target, never did return. Nine more good men lost.

Back at the hardstand I gathered up my things and jumped out the waist door. As I walked to where the crew was gathering for our ride in, I saw guys climbing all over #677, putting even more patches on her old body. Although she got us back in one piece… I hoped I'd never see her again… except in a museum, perhaps, where she really belonged.

Friday, February 16.
Mission number seven: Dortmund

Three days later the 327th would lead Fame's Favored Few on a mission to destroy a coking plant that made Benzol. The red line terminated in the eastern end of "Happy Valley," just northeast of Cologne, at the city of Dortmund. I had never heard of a coking plant and had no idea what Benzol was. But the briefing officer said this was a high priority target.

As always in "Happy Valley," flak was moderate on the IP, and many aircraft sustained battle damage, but the 92nd suffered no losses.

The landscape below was dotted with huge white storage tanks. That day I found out one thing about Benzol, if hit by a bomb, the storage tank and Benzol turned into a gigantic ball of fire. An awesome site.

Not only did we destroy the coking plant but most of the storage tanks went up with it. It was a great show. A job well done.

Tuesday, February 20.
Mission number eight: Nuremberg

In the 1930's, during the great depression, we used to save our precious nickels for the Saturday afternoon matinees. We walked about three miles to the old Eastwood theater on Seven Mile Road in Detroit. There was a bus, but we didn't have the fare.

Saturday matinees were cowboy movies, featuring guys like Tom Mix, Hopalong Cassidy, Ken Maynard, Tim McCoy and Gene Autry. There were always cartoons, a serial and the Movietone News. I never will forget my mother apologizing with a tear in her eye because she could only spare one penny for each of us to buy goodies with.

It was in the Movietone News that I first saw Adolph Hitler. Dressed in his SS uniform he created an atmosphere of hysteria ranting and raving in front of a backdrop of hundreds of Swastika flags. Searchlights filled the night as he shouted to hundreds of thousands of German youth. A shock of dark hair bounced off his forehead over one eye in tune with his wild gestures.

He whipped the multitudes to an emotional frenzy until they jumped to their feet, and with arms extended thundered, *Sieg Heil!* and *Heil Hitler!*

That took place in Nuremberg, and this morning I was reminded of those newsreels when the briefing officer said that Nuremberg would be our target today.

Nuremberg is due north of Munich, and lies in a wooded area known as the Middle Franconian Basin, on the river Pegnitz. The second largest city in Bavaria, it is also the capital of Franconia. It was one of the leading industrial cities in southern Germany, and it was... *a twenty-seven-eighty!*

We were flying a brand-new B-17G today. As I approached the aircraft the crew-chief fell in beside me and said that the chaff chute had not been installed yet. He asked if I wanted the box of chaff put on board. My first reaction was… why? But then I thought of the camera-well in the waist floor next to the ball turret and told him to put it there. This decision turned out to be one of the most important of my young life, and for our waist gunner, perhaps *the* most important.

Just before the bomb run I connected my oxygen hose to a walk around bottle and started toward the camera well. Les had been manning the gun on my side of the plane and I hadn't been able to see him because the bulkhead was in my way. But now, as I entered the waist, I saw him sitting with his back to the fuselage staring into space. His oxygen mask dangled on his chest and his face was a ghostly white. Because of the glassy look in his bloodshot eyes and his drooling blue lips I thought he was dead. It was apparent that he had become ill, removed his mask to regurgitate, and had been overcome by anoxia in the process.

I quickly pressed his mask to his face and thanked God that he hadn't thrown up in it. If he had, he never would have made it. With the other hand I turned his oxygen gauge to "PURE." Oxygen gauges were adjustable. We normally used a mixture of Nitrogen and other gasses. After a few moments he jerked violently; grabbed his mask with both hands; fiercely pressed it to his face, and was now inhaling pure oxygen. Soon he was back at his job scanning the skies for Bandits. Satisfied he was all right, I disconnected my walk around bottle, and thought that I had connected the hose of my mask to the spare gunner's position.

Straddling the camera well, I opened it, sat down, and started to throw out the chaff. Strangely, I felt flakes of ice hitting my face *inside* my mask, and at the same time I felt lightheaded. It suddenly dawned on me what was going on. I looked down and confirmed my suspicions. The flakes were ice crystals formed by the moisture in the hose of my mask. Apparently, during the excitement, I had not properly secured my hose to the main system and it was dangling on my chest. The two hoses were secured together by a twist lock that snapped into place. I grabbed the ends of both hoses, the one to the main system and the one on my mask, and tried to make the connection. But it was too late. Like a drunk that can't touch his nose, I couldn't make the ends meet. The waist gunner was standing with his back to me looking out the window for bandits. In one last desperate effort before I passed out, I leaned over, grabbed his pant leg and jerked. He turned, saw my predicament, and quickly secured my mask to the main system. In a few moments my recovery was complete. I gave Les the OK sign with my gloved right hand, he went back to his window, and I finished throwing out the chaff.

The mission was completed without further incident.

[When Hank Lapinski read this in 1995, he asked why I hadn't reported the incident to him. In retrospect, I told him I realize I should have, but at the time, since no one was hurt, I did not want to embarrass my comrade, or myself. Apparently, Les too, had no interest in reporting the incident.]

Thursday, February 22.
Mission number nine: Wittenberg

Apparently, there were some people in high places who opposed morale bombing such as *Thunderclap*. Instead they proposed an all-out bombing of military targets in or near small towns that had not yet been bombed. This strategy, called *Operation Clarion*, was planned to be carried out in two assaults, and the first, a *twenty-seven-eighty,* was scheduled for February 22.

"Gentlemen, today you will participate in the greatest air strike since the invasion of Normandy," the man in the briefing room said. It appeared there were two military objectives to *Operation Clarion*. One, to disrupt the German transportation network throughout Germany and Holland, and two, to find out if the Luftwaffe was still a viable force in this war. The Luftwaffe had rarely been seen since the Battle of the Bulge.

To accomplish the first objective, every available aircraft, more than 6,000, would bomb many targets at low altitudes for pinpoint accuracy. For the second, there would be *no* fighter escort, a challenge to the Luftwaffe. Our 'little friends' would spend the day seeking targets of opportunity on the ground.

"Your target for today is a road overpass at Wittenberg." The briefing officer was pointing to a town on the Elbe sixty miles southwest of Berlin [Martin Luther was born in Wittenberg].

"You will be going in at 12,000 feet." Normally we went in between 28,000 and 32,000 feet.

"Because of the nature of this mission," he continued, "and for all those new faces I see out there this morning, I'd like to remind you of 'Jerry's' latest brainstorms, the *Jet* and the *Bat*." Then he launched a commentary regarding the dangers and weaknesses of these new revolutionary aircraft. First he talked about the ME-262 Jet fighter-bomber. This jet propelled aircraft could travel at unheard of speeds of over six-hundred miles an hour and climb to altitudes higher than any other manned aircraft. At this particular time in history, with a skilled pilot behind the controls, it was the most formidable aircraft in the world.

[And therein lies the rub. It wasn't long before the lack of skilled pilots' would haunt Goering and end this aircrafts superiority. A rooky pilot in an ME-262 was hardly a match for a skilled pilot in a P-51. The ME-262 was originally designed as a fighter, but much to the dismay of the Luftwaffe, Hitler insisted that it be used as a bomber. First: Had Hitler not interfered with the original design of this amazing aircraft, which greatly delayed its production, and Second: If he had not canceled the Luftwaffe's "Operation "Herman" to launch his ill advised "Der Gross Schlag," in which he lost so many experienced pilots, the last months of the war would have been catastrophic for the Allied air forces. Fortunately, for us in particular, Hitler never thought in terms of defense. It was only after the "Battle of the Bulge" that he reluctantly allowed this aircraft to be used as a fighter.]

Then the man warned us of the ME-163 Komet, we called, the *Bat*. The *Bat* was a rocket propelled aircraft, almost all wing. It had a very limited range due to its voracious consumption of fuel. To conserve fuel the pilot fired it in very short bursts, gliding alternately. During that burst the *Bat* attained amazing speeds and reached incredible altitudes. But to be effective with its two 30MM cannons, it had to slow down to our air speed, and then it was just another fighter. The real danger was, if they should decide to use it as a Kamikazi, or suicide, plane... *And before the war ended, some German pilots did.*

⌘

I had heard all this before, and was amused that, first the man tells us we are going to be used as bait for the ME-262, the most formidable aircraft in the world. Then he says, look out for the *Bat* in case they were to use it as a Kamikazi. That was inspiring, if they were to use it as a Kamikazi it had the potential of wiping out most of a squadron. And those of us that knew better, knew there was no defense against that.

February 22, was a perfect day for flying. There wasn't a cloud in the sky. We called the mission a 'Cook's Tour.'

Over the 'Big Ditch' I swung the dial of my receiver to pick up some music as I often did now to ease the tension and boredom. I stopped when I heard Margaret Whiting singing *Dream*. When the recording was over a sexy female voice, said:

"And now here's Peggy Lee with, *Somebody Else is Taking My Place*." It was Axis Sally. After the Peggy Lee recording was finished Sally started delivering her Nazi propaganda.

"To all of you GI Joe's out there eating K rations and freezing to death," she said, "you can be sure of one thing, somebody else *is* taking your place. Some 4F is working overtime and making all that money and all those Jeeps, tanks and planes, to send over here for *you* to get killed in, *then,* he spends that money making *your* girl,"

When she was through, Lord Haw Haw, Chicago born Douglas Chandler, came on the air. He predicted that the British and Americans would soon sign an Armistice and help the brave German soldier save the world from Bolshevism.

"The Western Allies must realize that if the Bolsheviks are not stopped *here* and *now*, the red cancer will spread throughout the world," he said. "In the meantime, it's up to the brave heart of the German soldier to stop the Red Tide at the Oder."

⌘

We passed over Holland and entered Germany. Visibility was excellent and I could clearly see the countryside below. A tiny train caught my eye. It looked like a toy chugging through the dark-green pine forest. White smoke trailed the engine and billowed away, disappearing over the trees. Then I saw a silver flash against the green and recognized the tiny wings of a Mustang. It reminded me of the spider and the fly, I knew what would happen next, and sure enough it did. The little engine turned into an orange and red ball and all those tiny railroad cars piled up helter skelter behind it. The silver wings flashed again when the Mustang turned to find another target of opportunity.

The mission was a long one, but we returned to Podington with no casualties.

Friday, February 23.
Mission number ten: Kitzingen

The second *Clarion,* flown the next day, was also a low level 'Cook's Tour' and another *twenty-seven-eighty*. Our target was the railroad yards at *Kitzingen,* on the River Main, between Frankfort and Nuremberg.

The 92nd was one of the lucky groups to come out of this mission undamaged. Many Groups were not so lucky. The ME 262s came up with a vengeance. The next day the 'Cook's Tours' were over. It was back to high altitudes and fighter escorts. At least we found out where the Luftwaffe was. But, at the time, I wondered if the losses were worth it.

Saturday, February 24.
Mission number eleven: Hamburg

The port of Hamburg is one of the world's largest harbors. It extends almost twenty-five miles along the Elbe River, from the North Sea to Germany's second largest city, Hamburg. During World War II this city and harbor were essential to the German war effort, and its defenses ranked with the very best.

Captain Pilliod, of the 325th, was to lead the group today on another *twenty-seven-eighty*. Our Squadron Commander, Lt. Colonel Cox, was the VIP flying with Pilliod. Due to cloud cover over the target, a synthetic oil plant, we bombed by H2X. Flak was meager but accurate. Bombing results were not observed.

On the long trip home something didn't look quite right on our left wingtip. I stared at the spot for a long time but couldn't figure out what was wrong. No one else mentioned it so I thought I was seeing things. After landing I walked under the wing to investigate and was soon joined by the rest of the crew. We all stared up at a hole in the wingtip big enough to put your arm through. The hole was near the tip of the wing and just missed the wing tank. An 88MM shell had gone clean through our wing.

[When Hank Lapinski read this, he said that he could see the hole better than I could. But since there was nothing we could do about it he decided not to worry the crew, so he never mentioned it at the time.]

Antiaircraft shells were timed to go off at predetermined altitudes, not on contact. Had that shell had our altitude on it, it would have blown our wing off. Also, if it had hit a little closer to the fuselage, it would have put a hole in our gas tank. The tanks were self sealing, but not for a hole that big.

Since the shell had entered from below and exited through the top, the bottom of the hole was clean and the top was jagged, like someone had made the hole with a giant can opener. That's what had caught my eye.

Sunday, February 25.
Mission number twelve: Munich

This would be our *fourth* mission in as many days and our *sixth* consecutive *twenty-seven-eighty*. The red lines converged on *Munich*.

Yesterday our target was Germany's second largest city, today, it was their third. Munich is on the Isar River and is the capital of Bavaria, *and* the birthplace of the Nazi party. It is just north of Austria and the Alps, west of Czechoslovakia, and a long way from Podington.

The briefing officer's pointer followed an almost straight line running southeast from Podington to somewhere near Dover. Then it crossed the 'Big Ditch' and entered France near Calais. Next came a very long flight over France near the towns of Lille, Verdun, Nancy and Comar. The red line entered Germany over the Rhine somewhere between Basil, Switzerland, and Freiburg, Germany. We could not fly over a neutral country, so we would hug the Swiss border, on the German side, to Lake Constance.

I liked this route because, if for any reason up to this point we had to abort, we could land in friendly France or neutral Switzerland. But at Lake Constance came the tough part. The red line turned northeast toward Czechoslovakia, skirted Munich, and looped around the city. Once north of the city it turned southwest. Our bomb run came back over Munich on a direct line to Lake Constance. From the lake we would turn and go home the same way we came in.

⌘

It was another beautiful day as we crossed the "Big Ditch" and entered friendly France. The way I saw it we had no real worries until we reached Germany. My biggest problem until then would be to stay awake. It was a long boring flight. At long last we crossed the Jura Mountains and entered enemy territory. Switzerland was just off our right wing.

"There's Lake Constance out there at two o'clock," the navigator said from the nose. "What a beautiful sight," he added. I couldn't see anything at two o'clock from the radio room. My vision was restricted to seven o'clock, then clockwise to about eleven o'clock.

"Whoo-ee!" George exclaimed from the ball turret. "Look at those mountains. Is that the Alps?" he asked.

"That's the Alps all right, they're more than 16,000 feet high," Bob answered.

Near Augsburg we turned east toward Freising and our IP. We were passing just a few miles north of the now infamous Dachau, the first Nazi death camp.

Dachau ranked only behind Auschwitz and Buchenwald, making it Germany's third worst extermination camp. However, we knew nothing about that at the time.

Near Freising we turned almost due south. We were on our IP and following the Isar River right into Munich. We had a good tail wind and were coming up on the target fast, just the way you want it. My chaff was gone and my eyes were fixed on the bombs. The flak was intense. Shrapnel sprayed the aircraft. IPs like this seemed *much* longer than seven minutes.

"Come on, come on!" someone murmured over the intercom, "Let's get rid of these damn bombs and get the hell out of here!"And then I heard the words that I now dreaded as much as *twenty-seven-eighty*. Hank said we were going to do a *three-sixty*.

Some *three-sixties* were worse than others, and Munich was one of them. To take another terrible beating was bad enough, but this far from the base we would also use up precious fuel. Perhaps it wasn't the fault of the lead bombardier, but he was the only guy I could think of to blame, and just about then I could have wrung his neck.

After bouncing around in that flak for almost fifteen minutes now, the group was finally heading toward Lake Constance and home. This time the lake was off our left wing and I could see what Bob Johnson and Waldschmidt had been talking about. It *was* a breathtaking sight. A large body of blue-green water with a spectacular backdrop of pines and jagged snow capped mountains rising to the south and east. Lake Constance is by far the largest lake in Germany, the third largest in Central Europe and the second largest of the lakes bordering the Alps. Its shoreline is more than one-hundred-sixty miles long and borders three countries, Germany, Switzerland and Austria.

Off our left wing, flying the high squadron that day was the 327th, with Tom Shanahan. As I watched the spectacular view, I noticed black smoke coming from the engine of an aircraft in the 327th. Soon the prop stopped turning and I could see flames coming from the cowling. Then the aircraft started to fall down and away. It was far below when I sighted the first tiny chute. Then, one by one, I counted seven more. That left one guy still in there. I could hear someone saying, "Come on… jump, damn it, *jump!*" When we last saw those eight chutes, they were lazily floating toward the lake. We never did see the ninth chute.

Tom Shanahan, January 1945
Artist: Robert L Thornton

A few moments later another aircraft in the 327th peeled off and started down with one engine gone. It gradually disappeared. No chutes were sighted from that one.

I never knew what plane Tom was in, so whenever a plane went down in the 327th it always troubled me until we got back to the base.

At S-2 we learned that it was Lt. Chase's crew that had bailed out near Lake Constance. The other crew returned late after refueling somewhere in England near the 'Big Ditch.'

⌘

It was Sunday night and I knew that Tom would probably be in the Day Room writing letters. We often met there to chat and write. Sure enough, I found him sitting at a table near the fireplace. When I sat down, he stopped writing and re lit his pipe, it was always going out.

"Did they land in the lake?" I asked… they could have landed in Germany, the lake, or Switzerland. Tom's pipe finally showed a sign of life. He stopped puffing and said,

"They had two or three miles to drift… that tail wind could have carried them to the lake. If they didn't make it to the other side though, they wouldn't last long in that cold water."

We never did find out what happened to Lt. Chase's crew.

12

EXCEPT FOR "CHOW TIME," THE MOST IMPORTANT PART OF THE DAY WAS "MAIL CALL." Mail Call was done in many ways… here's the way it worked at Podington in 1945.

Someone from the Orderly Room would enter the barracks with a mail bag… or box, and yell "Mail Call." We would then gather around him in the middle of the room. After picking up a piece of mail he would call out the recipient's name. The recipient would identify himself with a "Here" or "Yo," and take his mail. Now, mail was a *very* serious business. When the man left, in most cases, the guys that were left empty handed usually went back to their bunks to sulk.

Then there were the "Dear John" letters. "Dear John" letters were from girl friends, fiancé's or wives… telling the recipient that it was all over. Some men did not take this news very well, and when one of our brethren received a letter like this, and we knew it, we kept an eye on him until he got over it. We didn't want him to do something stupid. The problem was, unfortunately, we didn't always know it.

One day I was hailed by the orderly room on the 'squawk box' and told to report to Colonel Cox, the 325th Squadron Commander. This is not good, I thought.

This was *not* SOP, Hank should come first... but Colonel Cox? That was skipping a level. When I entered the Orderly Room I knew the guy at the reception desk who, at the time, was busy typing, and I whispered... "What the heck does he want ME for?" "How the hell do I know, knock on his door and find out," was his response. I did, and I heard the Colonel say, "Come in." Once inside I snapped to attention, saluted, and said... "Sergeant Thornton, 368 765 69 reporting sir."

"At ease Sergeant," he said, as he reached over and pulled a letter out of a bunch of papers on his desk. After scanning the letter, he asked..."Sergeant... why don't you write your mother?"

"I do sir," then I added... "Often."

"I have a letter here that says she hasn't heard from you in months..."

"There must be some mistake, Sir, I write at least once a week."

He looked at the letter again, then asked..."Would you repeat your serial number Sergeant?"

I rattled off my serial number again. He then put the letter down, and smiled... "Well I'll be dammed, we've got two Thorntons here, and this ones not even in our squadron! Do you have a brother here?" I smiled back..."Not that I know of, Sir." Still smiling he said, "My mistake... go on, get out'a here Sergeant."

I liked Colonel Cox, and I'm proud to say that one day I flew a mission with him.

13

THE FALCON HOTEL DINNING ROOM, CASTLE
ASHBY, NORTHAMPTONSHIRE, FEBRUARY, 1945.

Annie and I were having tea after lunch.

*"I was only thirteen when my brother, flying a Spit
[Spitfire] went down over Kent, in The Battle of Britain.
He was so young... things have never been the same
since. She hesitated, fighting off tears in those beautiful
eyes. She paused to regain her composure.*

*"Anyway. . . we had a second home in London back
then. Dad had to be there because of his job. Mum and
I would go there on most week ends. One Saturday Dad
was tied up in Oxford, so we decided to have lunch and
do some shopping.*

*Just as we were stepping off the coach [bus], on
our way home, the air raid siren went off. There was
an underground station nearby, so we went into the
tube. After what seemed like an eternity of thumping,
rumbling and shaking, we heard the all clear.*

*When we stepped outside we were stunned. We
could plainly see that our end of the block had been
completely destroyed. We couldn't even get up there...*

the firemen had the road blocked off. We lost so many precious things in that house.

Luckily, the family pub, just a few blocks away, was unscathed and open. They had a wireless [radio] and said that all the train stations were untouched and running. Mum wanted to go home, and tried to call dad, but couldn't get through. Mum knew the man who owned the pub, and he said he would get a message to dad. Two hours later we were having tea with Fanny and Charley."

Before the war was over, in London alone, more than *400,000* civilians would die in air raids, and *one million* homes would be destroyed.

14

A Saturday Night Dance in February, Podington Air Base.

WHEN WE LANDED IN THE UK IN DECEMBER OF 1945, THERE WERE MANY MORE AVAILABLE WOMEN IN THE COUNTRY THAN MEN, AND MOST OF THE AVAILABLE MEN WERE YANKS. Therefore, wartime romances between English women and Yanks abounded. Many of these romances blossomed into marriage. But most just faded away. Each romance had a story all its own. Some leaving broken hearts, and even illegitimate children behind. This terrible war had promoted the mentality of... *"take what happiness you can find today, for tomorrow may never come."* And with that mentality... romantic interludes were inevitable. And it was just that kind of attitude that brought me to the dance this Saturday night.

When I first arrived in the UK, we were required to view army films about venereal disease. They really worked on me, so I had avoided sex like the plague... and there was much to be had. But believe me, for a nineteen-year-old, with lots of testosterone, that was a very difficult thing to do. Then, this Saturday, it hit me. Since I had been here, the 92nd had lost almost one whole squadron. At that rate, I figured I would never reach the ripe old age of twenty. Right then and there I decided to change my policy of "no sex." And since there was a dance tonight, I thought that was a good place to start.

About every other week the group held dances in a hanger and bussed women in from surrounding communities. In the past I had always found these dances rather stressful, because the only dance I could do was a fox trot, and I couldn't do that very well. I never owned a zoot suit, and couldn't do the boogie woogie. So if I asked, and the young lady said yes, I was afraid of making a fool of myself. On the other hand, if she said no, I had this overpowering fear of being rejected. It was a catch 22, so, in the past I never asked. But tonight, I knew I had to go that extra yard and do it.

These dances were always the same. When the ladies arrived, all the guys were already on one side of the hanger. So the gals took over the other side. The band and refreshments were against a wall at the far end of the hanger. The first dance of the evening was always awkward. Both sides would give each other the once over until some brave guy broke the ice. After that, most barriers broke down and soon many couples were dancing... except for me and a few other wallflowers. But tonight I was determined to make things change.

Like most Saturday night dances, there was a young lady out there that got my attention, and, as usual, I was trying my best to muster up enough courage to approach her. This just happened to be my lucky night. She caught me staring at her, and when our eyes met, she didn't look away. As every male out there over five must know, when a female gives a man that certain look, sometimes it can work just like a magnet. It's called a 'come hither' look. And I had just gotten a 'come hither look.' Now, that look gave me the courage I needed, and I made my move. When I told the young lady I was a lousy dancer, she said something like, "Well I'm not, so I'll give you a lesson." And that's how I met Annie.

Slightly over five foot… perhaps five two or three, from the top of her head to the tips of her toes… she was all female. As I awkwardly followed her instructions she quickly put me at ease with her good humor, dazzling smile, and tantalizing eyes. I was totally captivated by her, and before the evening was over, I was doing a pretty good Fox Trot and had her phone number. It was a dream come true. I never will forget the last thing she said to me that evening as she gave me her phone number.

"Here… now you *will* knock me up won't you?" It's a good thing I was warned that the American interpretation of that statement was… "Here… now you *will* call me won't you?"After I saw her off on the bus, I felt like dancing all the way back to the barracks, and now believed in love at first sight. I was smitten with the fever. Suddenly, all the army movies about VD were history.

Before our first date I had talked to her on the phone at least four times… flew five missions, and had been awarded another air medal. After the Munich mission I had three days off and we arranged to meet for tea at a restaurant in a small village about half way between her home and Podington. Annie told me that she lived in the country, not far from Northampton, our 'Liberty Run' town.

We were both coming by bike. I remember it well because, even though I wore long underwear and my full dress woolen uniform, I nearly froze to death. But wild horses couldn't have kept me away. I was early, and nervously sipping tea when she arrived. She looked around the room, and when our eyes met and she smiled, my heart skipped a beat. Her windblown auburn hair framed a face so pretty it almost made me melt. She was even prettier than I remembered.

As we made small talk over tea, I was mesmerized by her smile, her rosy cheeks and those enchanting eyes. It was a good thing she couldn't read my mind, for, as we talked I had this yearning that I wanted to make another Annie, just like her.

From the restaurant we went to her home for a pre arranged lunch with her mother. English homes were not new to me, I had often hitchhiked in this area and had never been passed by. My biggest problem had been to politely get away from the people that gave me a ride. They all wanted to take me home for tea and have me meet their families and friends. Their curiosity about Americans seemed endless.

When Annie said she lived in the country she really meant it. Her home [or estate] was nestled in a gated wooded area well back from the road. There were several smaller buildings behind the main house. I learned later that she was very good with horses, and the longer of the buildings was a stable. Before the war, her father's hobby was raising horses. In those days, she said, the stable was full, but all that remained now were three riding horses and Charley, a grizzled seventy-year-old groom and handy man.

The two story main house was well furnished and spacious. It was vintage British, with no central heat. Every room had a fireplace. Hard coal was used to fuel the fireplaces and cook stoves in the kitchen. However, coal was in short supply because of the war, and was rationed. They used it only in the kitchen, dining and living rooms. Those three rooms were the only warm rooms in the house in the winter months. Therefore, everyone wore sweaters and used lots of blankets at night. I noticed a 'wireless' in just about every room. They were all tuned to the BBC news most of the time. That way they could receive the latest news and early warnings of air raids.

Not long ago, I thought, I was nailing tops on boxes of roller-bearings in Detroit, and had never been more than two hundred miles from home. Now, in a foreign land, on the other side of a vast ocean, I was getting a tour of this magnificent home by this gorgeous creature. And to think, if I had been rejected because of my flat feet, I probably would still be nailing tops on boxes.

Lunch was served by Fanny, the live-in housemaid. Fanny was Charley's wife, and they lived in the servant's quarters just off the main house. I could see where Annie got her good looks. Her mother was beautiful. If she could take a few years off, they could pass for twins. Her mother had been to America once. She accompanied her husband to New York on a business trip before America entered the war. After lunch Annie guided me to Northampton where I checked into a small inn, more like a Bed and Breakfast. Then we went to the market square and browsed in the shops. A personnel carrier [Liberty-Run bus] from the 92nd Bomb Group was parked in the square. They ran every hour on the hour from 7AM until 11PM. My safety valve, if need be. This was also the more conventional way that I usually came to town.

We returned to Annie's that evening for dinner where I met her father. I found him to be rather constrained, nothing like Annie or her mother. He was a distinguished looking man, well educated and obviously a man of means. He was very reserved and somewhat stuffy, I thought. My first impression of him was that he did not consider Americans as equals. I thought he tolerated *me* only because he had to, to keep peace in the family. All

I found out about him, and not from him, is that he had something to do with the war effort that was very hush-hush. He spent most of his time at Oxford, but also had a flat [apartment] in London. This happened to be one of the rare days when he was home.

The next day when I returned, Annie and I toured the countryside. Then we stopped at the Falcon Hotel in Castle Ashby, where we spent a leisurely lunch getting better acquainted. I learned that some of her girlfriends had twisted her arm that Saturday night, and that was the first time she had come to one of our dances. She was born in London; once had a house there; was eighteen; had gone to private schools; had studied ballet since she was six but had recently given it up. After the war, her father was expecting her to go to Oxford, but she preferred Cambridge. The only trouble with Cambridge was, she said, women could not get a degree there. However, she thought that would soon change.

She had had an older brother in the RAF who flew Spitfires, but he was shot down in 'The Battle of Britain.' The family took his death very badly, particularly Annie. They were very close.

As for the Americans? At first her father thought you were crazy with your daylight bombing. He thought your losses would be so great your Congress would put a stop to it. But now, everyone is cheering you on… as they put it, *"you were giving it to 'em back."*

When asked if she ever had a serious romance, she said, "How could I, until you Yanks came along there weren't many boys left to have a romance with. Then there was ballet; school; the war; and my father," she added.

"What about your father?" I asked.

"I'm a 'Daddy's little girl.' If he had his way I'd be locked in my room until I was an old maid."

When asked if her father disliked Yanks, she was very perceptive. "No. He was very much in favor of getting Yanks over here in the first place. But, when it comes to *me*, he gets prudish, and *very* protective. It doesn't matter if you're a Yank or not, if that's what you're asking. He has his own plans for my future. But, I have plans of my own. Don't let him scare you."

Annie and I soon became an item. Now, when I was a thousand miles behind enemy lines, it was comforting to know that someone back there was waiting for me. Someone who cared. She was my first love, and she shattered the image I had of the English. I had always thought they were cool and reserved, rarely showing their emotions. Annie was anything but. She was very affectionate, and not afraid to show it. I soon found out that, after what happened to her brother, Annie more or less got what Annie wanted. And to my good fortune, at that time in her life, she wanted me. I always felt that her mother liked me too. It wasn't long before Annie convinced her to let me sleep in one of the spare bedrooms whenever I was in town overnight. I'm sure her father didn't like this arrangement. But after that first day, he was rarely home when I was there anyway.

15

WHILE I HAD BEEN ON LEAVE, THE 327th LED THE ENTIRE 8th AIR FORCE TO BERLIN. About an hour out of Berlin Lt. John Paul, Tom Shanahan's pilot, lost his number two engine. He could have bombed a target of opportunity and come home, but he elected to continue on alone and bomb Berlin at 15,000 feet. That took a lot of guts, and earned Lt. Paul's crew 'The Crew of the Week' award.

This is "CREW OF THE WEEK' picture of Lt. Paul's crew. The only man I knew well on this crew was my good friend, Tom Shanahan who gave me the picture, (bottom row, second from left). Lt. Paul must be one of the two officers in the top row.

Not so fortunate that day, was the crew of Lt. Mason of the 326th Squadron. Lt. Mason lost two engines over Berlin and never did return.

Thursday, March 1.
Mission number thirteen: Reutlingen

On March 1st we went back to work. We were scheduled to fly our *thirteenth* mission and *seventh* consecutive *twenty-seven-eighty*. It would be a very unusual mission. The 92nd would lead the First Wing of the 8th Air Force, and Captain Pilliod would lead the 92nd again. Colonel Wilson would be the VIP at Pilliod's side. This would be the Captain's last mission. He was completing his tour today.

Our target was the marshaling yards in *Reutlingen.* This city is just south of Stuttgart in southern Germany, almost as far as Munich. 'Recon' [reconnaissance] photos later showed that we hit the target with excellent results. The passenger and freight stations were practically destroyed. We saw no flak, but, not long after leaving the target area we heard a cry from George Waldschmidt in the ball turret.

"BAT... NINE O'CLOCK!" I looked out and picked him up. We had never seen a real *Bat* before. He was out of our range, but one of our Mustangs was in pursuit. Just when the Mustang pulled close enough to fire, the *Bat* shot up and away like a streak of lightning, leaving our 'little friend' to eat his contrail. At about 40,000 feet, far above the Mustang's ceiling, he slowly rolled and lazily performed acrobatics on his way down. I actually believe he was showing off.

But then he electrified everyone. He pointed his nose *directly* at the 325th leading the wing, and hurtled through our formation like a tracer bullet. He literally *shot* past our left wing. Some said later that he was firing at us. If he was, I missed that part. I always believed that he decided to play Kamakazi, and take out our Group Leader with as many other aircraft as he could, but either 'chickened out,' or just plain missed.

Friday, March 2

The next morning Hank's crew was ordered to report to our Operations Officer. When we arrived at his office we were ushered in by his orderly, but the man wasn't there. The orderly left and closed the door.

We silently wandered around the room, bewildered. Soon the door opened and the 'Ops' officer briskly entered. Everyone jumped to attention. He quickly walked behind his desk and sternly said, "at ease." There was no mistaking his mood. Something was very wrong. We were obviously not going to receive any medals.

He then soberly recited a litany of complaints regarding our crew. Among other things, he chastised the gunners for not firing at the *Bat* as it swept through our formation yesterday. I couldn't understand that, that Bat was going so fast *no one* could have fired at it. But this was the army, and there was no arguing with a superior officer. All we could do was stand there and take his dressing down.

Later in the day, much to my surprise, I was promoted to Tech. Sergeant [T/Sgt.] Three stripes and two rockers. The highest rank an ROMG could achieve. Evidently I wasn't one of the guys the 'Ops' officer was unhappy with.

There was no celebration though, shortly after my promotion, the day was marred with the news that the group lost one aircraft and one crewman that afternoon. While on a practice mission over England, a plane in the 407th caught fire. The pilot called for a bail out and the tail gunner was killed when his chute failed to open.

Saturday, March 3.
Mission number fourteen: Chemnitz

This was going to be my *ninth* consecutive *twenty-seven-eighty*. Our primary target was an oil refinery in the city of Ruhland, Bavaria. However, because of bad weather, we were unable to pick up the primary target. We then sought out our secondary, the city of *Chemnitz,* now called Karl-Marx-Stadt.

This was a very long mission, more than ten hours. The target was near Czechoslovakia. Everything had gone very well and we were almost home free near Brussels when two aircraft in the 327th collided. Unlike the first collision on my third mission, I saw this one. I numbly watched as the terrible sight unfolded not knowing if Tom was in there. One Fortress broke up in pieces, which then fluttered and plummeted out of sight. The other disappeared in a spin.

Our losses for the day were two aircraft and eighteen crewmen. One chute had been sighted. But much to my relief, Tom's ship was not among them.

16

March 4,5,6.
A three day pass at Annie's

*S*UNDAY, MARCH 4. Annie and I boarded a train in Wellingborough and were in London an hour later. Annie knew her way around the city, having spent most of her childhood here. Her father maintained a flat here ever since their house was destroyed in The Battle of Britain. We were here today because she was taking me to Madam Tussaud's Wax Museum.

After lunch we walked to the underground to catch a train to the Museum. As we stood waiting, the cement platform slapped my feet, and I felt my ears pop, then I heard a rumble. I looked at Annie and she simply said, *"That... was a V2."*

When the train pulled into the station and we left the tube near Madam Tussaud's, we saw a huge mushroom of dust off in the distance. Annie was used to this, as were most Brits. She was a seven-year war vet and had survived I don't know how many bombing raids, Buzz Bomb attacks, and V2 rocket strikes. And today she was not going to let a V2 stop her from showing me Madam Tussaud's. There was nothing you could do about a V2 rocket strike if it had your name on it anyway.

Monday, March 5

Monday we spent a typical day at home whenever I stayed overnight. After a hearty breakfast of oatmeal, tea and kippered herring [on some days it was duck eggs and toast with marmalade] Annie, Charley and I, gave the horses a work out and rubdown. I had been riding horses in Michigan since I was fourteen and thought I was good at it, but soon found out I was just a novice compared to Annie and Charley.

As we roamed the nearby fields and woods, Annie led the way. She occasionally wore a riding outfit on such occasions, and was absolutely stunning on a horse. The girl and mount were poetry in motion, they seemed to be made for each other. There was something very sexy about it.

While Annie and I were roaming through town later, I bought myself a pair of riding boots I intended to leave at her house. I was going to take Charley up on his offer made earlier today to give me riding lessons. [Northampton was, and still is, the boot and shoe manufacturing capital of the UK.]

⌘

Just about everybody had their favorite local pub, and just about everybody knew everybody at those pubs. In the evenings someone always played the piano. They sang songs, played darts, chess, checkers, or just talked. Warm Mild and Bitter beer, Ginger beer, Stout, Ale, Guinness and Gin, were popular drinks.

During most daylight hours Annie and her mother did volunteer work, and there was a great need for that.

But, in the evenings, sitting around reading and listening to the BBC on the radio could sometimes get boring. So Annie's mother had occasionally taken to visiting her neighborhood pub. She liked her Guinness, and mixing with the townspeople. [Her husband preferred his all male club in London.] Sometimes, when I was staying overnight Annie and I would go with her.

The first time I went was Monday evening, and I was the only Yank in the place. Annie and her mother knew most everyone there. The first drink I ordered was a Scotch and water. When I finished that, the waitress served me another without my asking. She pointed to a patron across the room who gave me Winston Churchill's famous "V" for victory sign and said, "Cheers Yank." And that happened almost every time I was in that pub. It got so bad that I had to learn how to stretch my drinking out to stay sober. Which didn't always work.

What I didn't know at the time was, that Scotch was very hard to come by in the war years. But… the lady who owned the pub had her own private stock that she only broke out on special occasions. I was flattered to learn later, that, whenever I came to her pub, she considered it a "special occasion."

I learned later that some of the people buying me drinks called me Annie's boy friend, and they *all* knew that I flew combat with the 92nd Bomb Group. Living so close to our base, many considered us family. Some watched the group assemble and leave in the morning. Then counted our aircraft as we returned. If they didn't get a full count they were saddened, wondering if they knew any of the men who were missing.

Pubs closed very early. You always knew it was closing time when the piano player began "I'll Be

Seeing You," and everyone joined in and sang. A very fitting and romantic song in those days.

Sometimes, on those particular evenings, we would stop at a take out restaurant and get some fish and chips [deep-fried fish and French fries] wrapped in the daily newspaper. Paper bags were another casualty of the war. Back at Annie's, we would open the paper on the kitchen table, Fanny would serve tea, and we, including Charley and Fanny, sat around listening to the BBC, talking and eating off the paper.

Tuesday, March 6

The next morning she took me to what she called her "Secret Place." It was a beautiful little pond fed by a brook and surrounded by trees. We sat on a grassy knoll on one side of the pond. It was here that she spent many happy hours reading and day dreaming while she grew up, she said. And, it was here that we spent many romantic hours in the coming weeks.

17

Wednesday, March 7.
Mission number fifteen: Fulda

IF YOU LOOK AT A MAP OF GERMANY, YOU WILL FIND THE CITY OF FULDA JUST NORTHEAST OF FRANKFORT ON THE BANKS OF THE RIVER IT'S NAMED AFTER.

Fulda was a target of opportunity on March 7. We encountered bad weather over our primary target and then experienced a technical failure in our PFF equipment over our secondary target. Fulda was on our list of "opportunities" and the skies were clear over that city, so we bombed it.

We suffered one casualty. A man in the 407th was wounded by flak. This mission broke my streak of consecutive *twenty-seven-eighties* at *nine*.

Thursday, March 8.
Mission number sixteen: Essen

According to the 325th load list [APO 557], signed by our Operations Officer, Captain Victor Cherback Jr. on March 8, 1945, I flew with Lt. Hank Lapinski on a mission to Essen in aircraft # 43-38877 Q. Due to some clerical error, I was never credited with this mission on my service record. A copy of the above load list was given to me by the 92nd Archivist Bob Elliot, and can be found with my service records. Although I didn't know it at the time, this would be my last mission on Lapinski's crew.

⌘

That evening, after returning from the Essen mission, there was a notice on the bulletin board stating: Effective immediately, Flight Engineer George Jaeger and ROMG Robert L. Thornton, were transferred to Albert T. Vermeire's Deputy Lead crew. And, the man I was replacing on Vermeire's crew, J. Robert Johnson, [not related to Lapinski's Bombardier] was transferred to Norwood D.Ringsred's Squadron Lead crew. It also stated that Ted Fossberg, Lapinski's bombardier, was also transferred to Ringsred's crew.

George, Ted and I were now in the *"Lead Pool."* A kind of promotion without a rank or pay increase. Each squadron had a Group Lead crew, a Squadron Lead crew, and a Squadron Deputy Lead crew. Squadrons took turns leading the group, and since there were four squadrons, that meant that each squadron led the group *every fourth mission*. Group Lead crews *only* flew when their squadron led the group, so they *only flew* every fourth mission.

Squadron Lead crews led the squadron on *every* mission they flew, *except* when their squadron led the group. When that happened, they flew *Deputy to the Group Lead*.

Squadron Deputy Lead crews also flew Deputy Lead on *every* mission *except* when their squadron led the group. When that happened, they flew in the number four position of the lead element. If the Group Lead were to get knocked out, the Squadron Lead would move up and take over the group, and the deputy lead would move out of the number four position and become the new deputy group lead. And he would also then become the new squadron lead.

[Every man's life on a combat crew depended on every other man on that crew doing his job. And the better he did it, the better the chance of survival. Every man wanted to be on a good crew, and men in the "Lead Pool" knew they were in a unique esprit de corps.]

Friday, March 9.
Mission number seventeen: Kassel

Just before our preflight inspection, we all gathered around the nose of the aircraft we were flying that day, and the new guys shook hands with Al Vermeire and his crew. I had seen these guys around before, but really didn't know them.

The other men on Al's crew were; Lt. Becker, Copilot; Lt. Maher, navigator; Staff Sgt. Stefel, waist gunner; Staff Sgt. Crowbar, ball turret gunner; and, Staff Sgt. Harmon, tail gunner. I believe Harmon had credit for one and one half ME-109's. Why the one half? Because if two men fired at the plane that went down at the same time, they each got credit for one half.

After preflight we boarded and were on our way. My first mission with Al Vermeire was to Kassel, on the

Fulda River. Smack dab in the center of Germany. Our target was a truck factory in that city.

Leading the 325th today was Lt. Ringsred. As his deputy, we were flying off his right wing.

Flak was moderate and accurate over the target. After we dropped on the truck factory, as on most missions, I watched the black puffs of flak as they seemed to float by my window. These puffs you see can't hurt you. You never see the burst that does. As I watched, a new box exploded nearby. It was so close I felt the aircraft bounce from the concussion. That burst caught an aircraft in the 327th with a direct hit. The pieces flew out of a big black cloud and disappeared. In seconds it was over. The plane, crew, everything was gone. They never knew what hit them. I prayed that my friend was not in that plane, and... for the men who were.

Hours later we were in the landing pattern at Podington. Three aircraft were shooting off red flares. Besides losing one aircraft and nine men in that barrage, three men were wounded. Two of those men were in the 325th. Lt. Joe Diamond, a navigator, was creased in the forehead by a piece of shrapnel and was scarred for life. [Joe and I would share many experiences as crew members in the coming months.]

The other, was my neighbor in the barracks again, Mel. Mel had survived a crash landing, a bail out over France when his aircraft broke up, and now, on his last mission, some fragments of flak penetrated his bucket seat and peppered him in his backside. Surgeons were able to extract everything but a tiny piece lodged in one testicle. As for my friend Tom Shanahan… he and his crew were home safe and sound. They had dodged another bullet.

Sunday, March 11.
Mission number eighteen: Bremen

Bremen, on the Weser River, in Lower Saxony, is Germany's second largest seaport, and is also the beginning of *The Fairy Tale Road,* immortalized by the Brothers Grim. Unfortunately, it was also the home of a large complex of submarine pens… and our target for the day.

The 325th was the high squadron today, and we pulled up to Ringsred's right wing, on my second mission with Lt. Vermeire.

Everything was going fine… until about an hour before the IP. Then something went wrong, and our number two engine went dead… but the prop was still spinning. It was actually, what we called, 'running away.'

This engine was right next to the radio room, and I could see, and feel it shaking. If Vermeire couldn't stop it, it could eventually wrench the engine right off the wing, or worse. In such cases, the pilot would try to 'Feather' the prop. If he was successful, we would only lose the use of the engine, but it would still be there.

Then, we were suddenly out of formation and going down in a steep dive. Now the whole plane was vibrating and shaking. I grabbed my chute, hooked it to my harness and waited for Al to order a bail out, which I expected to hear any moment now.

The plane shook and rattled so hard I thought that every nut and bolt was about to shear off. I felt like I weighed a ton, and feared I would soon experience the same feeling of helplessness as described to me by Mel, the one airman I knew that had survived such a circumstance. As you may recall, Mel was saved when the aircraft broke up and he found himself in midair.

Just as I was about to go for the waist door and bail out, the intercom clicked on and Al said something like... "Don't worry guys, we'll get this bird under control." He sounded so calm and sure of himself that I completely relaxed. And sure enough, after what seemed like a lifetime, I saw the number two prop stop, and we smoothed out and leveled off. After that I always thought that Al Vermeire could walk on water.

We had lost one engine and a lot of altitude. The group was nowhere in sight, then Al said we were going to bomb Bremen anyway. Of course I had no choice, but just about then I would have followed Al Vermeire anywhere. As we approached the target alone, flak was bursting all around us. We were so low I could see fire trucks down there. Firefighters were desperately trying to extinguish the flames of burning buildings created by our group just ahead of us. We dropped our bombs and were soon on our way home.

[The following is the official United States Army Air Force version of what happened to us that day as it appeared on every bulletin board on the base under a picture of our crew. I obtained this copy from Al Vermeire himself, after a telephone conversation in January 1995.]

"CREW OF THE WEEK"

On 11 March 1945, 2nd Lt. Albert T. Vermeire and crew flew in the Deputy Lead position of the High Squadron of the 40th "C" Group on a mission to Bremen, Germany. One hour before the IP, while the formation was climbing to bombing altitudes, the No. 2 engine of Lt. Vermeire's aircraft developed mechanical trouble and went dead. Unable to continue the climb with the group with only three good engines, Lt. Vermeire was forced out of formation. Difficulty was encountered in feathering the propeller of the defective engine for some fifteen minutes. When finally the racing propeller was feathered, Lt. Vermeire had the choice of continuing on to the target alone or bombing a target of opportunity, an act that would have, under the

Top Row: (of crew picture) Lt's. Becker (CP), Maher (N) and Vermeire (P). Bottom Row: Sgt's. Stefel (WG), Crowbar, (BTG) Jaeger (ETG), Thornton (ROMG), and Harmon (TG). The crew chief of the aircraft was M/Sgt McCartney. (Aircraft is #354 "Little Runt.")

circumstances, been perfectly permissible. He chose the former more difficult course. Dropping down to 17,000 feet in order to conserve the power of his three remaining engines, Lt. Vermeire and his crew continued toward the submarine pens of Bremen. They bombed the target on the smoke markers of previous groups. By going over the target at what was comparatively so low an altitude, they exposed themselves to more than the usual danger from flak. However, the aircraft escaped unscathed through the moderate flak and Lt. Vermeire was able to intercept the group on the return route and return safely to base with the formation. The resolution and courage displayed by Lt. Vermeire and his crew on this mission are highly commendable and reflect credit upon themselves, their squadron, and the group.

[This is the second omission on my service record. This official account, above, has been confirmed by Al Vermeire, the pilot, and Bob Elliot, the 92nd Bomb Group Archivist. This gives me twenty-seven missions, not the twenty-five as shown on my service record]

Monday, March 12.
Mission number nineteen: Swinemunde

There was an explosion of expletives in the briefing room as the curtain was pulled and the man's pointer came to rest on the far right-hand side of the map. It was near the Pomeranian Bay, on the Baltic Sea, and not far from the border of Poland. In fact, it was also *very* close to Russia. And, of course, it was a *twenty-seven-eighty.*

"Your target for today, gentlemen, is the dock area at *Swinemunde*," the man said. "You will be dropping one hundred pound anti personnel bombs in tactical support of Marshall Rokossovky's White Russian Armies."

At this point someone in the back of the room asked, "Is this trip really necessary?" The officer smiled and waited for the laughter to subside, then continued.

"Since this is a deep penetration raid, fuel consumption is critical…"

The 325th, with Lt. Bekker and crew, was leading the entire group today. That put Squadron Leader Ringsred in the Deputy Lead spot, and Al Vermeire and crew in the number four position. We started our IP over the Pomeranian Bay in the Baltic Sea, approaching Swinemunde from the north. Flak was moderate and accurate. Shortly after 'bombs away' Ringsred lost an engine and aborted. We then moved up and took over his place as Group Deputy Lead.

The last word heard from Ringsred was that he was landing at Malmo, Sweden, with a wounded man on board. That meant that he and his crew would be interned for the rest of the war. And that meant the war was over for my comrade on Lapinski's original crew, Bombardier Ted Fossberg, and the ROMG who I replaced on Vermeire's crew, J. Bob Johnson. You might recall that Ted *almost* went to Sweden on February 3rd.

Al Vermeire now became our new Squadron Leader, and I was now Squadron Lead ROMG. Since Ringsred's engineer was our barracks chief, I also replaced him, and moved into the only private room in the barracks.

Wednesday, March 14.
Mission number twenty: Lohne

Today the 326th Group Lead crew of Captain Hoffman, with Lt. Colonel Hardin flying as the VIP, would lead the Wing to bomb a rail yard at Lohne. This was another mission to disrupt major transportation centers, and it was a success. This was our first mission as the 325th

Squadron Lead crew. Extreme damage was inflicted on the whole yard. The passenger station and roundhouse were destroyed, trains were derailed, and much of the track was gone. The 92nd suffered no losses or injuries.

Saturday, March 17.
Mission number twenty-one: Molbis

Saturday our bomb bay was loaded with five-hundred pound bombs, and our mission was to destroy another Benzol plant. This plant was near the city of Molbis. It was our second mission as Squadron Leader, and at the MPI something went terribly wrong. We were well into the bomb run; my chaff was all gone; I was sitting in my bucket seat with my eyes glued to the bombs… and I was stunned by what I saw next. Before the bombardier finished saying "bombs away," I watched them fall. It happened in a fraction of a second… they were all gone but one. *The bottom bomb on the right hand side of the rack was still out there.*

In the cockpit, Al was waiting for me to repeat "bombs away," so he could close the bomb bay doors, instead, I had to tell him we had a bomb hung up out there. This was a very serious problem. We couldn't close the doors until we got rid of that bomb, nor could we stay with the group. Someone *had* to go out there on that catwalk and get rid of that bomb, and it couldn't be done at 28,000 feet. There was no oxygen out there, and it was 60 degrees below zero. That meant we had to go down to 10,000 feet where a man could breathe, and not freeze.

After I gave Al the bad news there was a short conference in the cockpit, which ended with Al giving Jaeger the job of getting rid of the bomb. Then I heard

George say that he would need help. I cringed at Al's response. I heard him say, *"Did you hear that Thornton, you're elected."* I clicked my throat mike to ON and said, "Roger."Although I really didn't *want* to go out there on that cat walk with the bomb bay doors open, I knew that I was the logical choice. And I couldn't let my good friend George go out there alone. We had been to hell and back together many times. This would just be one more time.

As Al was taking us down to 10,000 feet so we could go out on the cat walk without oxygen, George told me that he would defuse the bomb, then pry it with a gun barrel that he would take from one of the flexible guns in the nose. He wanted me to brace my back against the bomb rack, then help push the bomb out with my foot.

Once Al leveled off at 10,000 feet, I took off my oxygen mask, snapped on my chest pack chute and moved to the doorway to look the situation over. With our air speed somewhere around one hundred-fifty MPH it was *very* windy out there. I couldn't resist the temptation to look down at the German countryside. It was farmland, and looked like a huge quilt. Different colored patches, some freshly plowed for spring planting. There were also some farm houses and barns scattered here and there.

In order to get to the bomb rack, I would have to go out there in that wind and traverse the narrow catwalk that led to the bomb rack and cockpit. There were ropes similar to those used in theater lobbies on each side of the narrow catwalk to help me keep my balance. We had all been on this cat walk many times, but never air born with the bomb bay doors open. If we should hit some turbulence, and lurched, or I lost my balance, I would experience my first parachute jump.

Then I remembered something they told us in our indoctrination about walking out of Germany. *If you ever find yourself in the Hinterland [like we were flying over right now] by all means, avoid young boys. Most young boys were members of the Hitler Youth. And they could have shotguns. Their big sport was hunting downed airmen… And they never took one alive.*

George interrupted my thoughts as he stepped out of the cockpit and closed the door. He had removed his helmet and his blond hair was blowing in the wind. The gun barrel was under one arm. He waved at me to come over.

I never hesitated. By now I had learned some secrets of performing under great duress. [1] Give your *total* concentration to the task at hand. [2] Use your basic instincts, *without thinking of the danger*. [3] If something bad is going to happen, it's going to happen to some other guy… In that state of mind I traversed the narrow catwalk to the bomb rack.

George was pointing to the dents in the bomb. We couldn't hear each other because of the noise of the engines, so we used hand signals. I shook my head in the affirmative, I had seen the other bombs make those dents. It looked as if someone had bashed it with a ball-peen hammer. George then kneeled on the catwalk, wrapped his left arm over the rope for support, then defused the bomb with his left hand while holding the gun barrel in his right… The bomb was now deactivated. Then, looking me in the eye, he nodded and started prying.

Pressing my back against the bomb rack, I pushed as hard as I could with my right foot. At first I thought the five-hundred pound monster would never let go. Then it suddenly gave way and was gone.

I looked at George, and for a brief moment our eyes met. The look that passed between us said it all. We were now members of a mutual admiration society. Smiling broadly, we exchanged a friendly salute and returned to our positions.

Seconds later German farmers must have been shocked when a five-hundred pound dud landed nearby. That is… if it didn't *land* on one of those farmhouses.

The bomb bay doors were already closing as I latched the door shut, and settled into my bucket seat. It took Al a couple of hours to climb back up to 28,000 feet and catch up with the group, in the meantime, we were a straggler… a sitting duck, and we kept our eyes peeled for Bandits. But we safely caught up with the group and returned to Podington.

That same day the Ludendorff bridge collapsed at Remagen. It was too late for the Germans though, a solid beachhead had been established on their side of the bridge.

Sunday, March 18.
Mission number twenty-two: Berlin

We were bumped to the Deputy Lead spot today, since the 325th was leading the group. And when that happened Lt. Bekker's Group Lead Crew took over. Flying with Lt. Bekker as the VIP today was our Squadron Commander, Lt. Colonel Cox.

When the Briefing Officer pulled back the curtain, we could see the red line running right to the "Big B." But unlike the February 3rd mission… I had no qualms about going on this mission. Being the Squadron Lead Radio Operator, with over twenty missions under my belt, certainly had something to do with it. I was now a veteran that had earned the respect of my comrades and today we were second in command taking the

whole group to one of the most feared targets in
Germany. As Deputy Lead we were also second in line
for take off... right behind Bekker. There were thirty-
four planes lined up behind us. We got off the ground
safely, pulled in on Bekker's right side, and started the
assembly. Climbing and circling, one by one, the rest of
our Squadron assembled around us. As we continued to
climb and circle, the High Squadron assembled to our
left. Followed by the Low Squadron to our right. Finally
Colonel Cox checked with the other two Squadrons and
we were ready. We struck out for the North Sea and the
"Big B."

Over Berlin the flak was intense and accurate. An
aircraft in the 407th with an engine on fire went into a
dive right over the center of the city. Just after the MPI,
Lt. Culver, of the 325th, dropped back with one engine
gone and another with the prop running away. Some
of those men were barracks mates. As I watched them
disappear I thought of stories I had heard of enraged
civilians hanging airmen to the nearest lamp-pole with
their own parachute shrouds.

We heard many reports of "Bandits" in the area, but
somehow they overlooked the 92nd. Back at Podington
we learned that the aircraft in the 407th had miraculously
extinguished the fire in their dive and landed in Russian
occupied Warsaw. They were back in Podington the
following week.

*[That day, March 18, 1945, the 8th Air Force
lost thirty-six bombers over Germany. That is the
equivalent of one whole group. The ME-262 Jet had
come up in full force for the first time, and shot down
twenty-seven of those bombers. Nine were victims of
anti aircraft fire. Over three-hundred-fifty crewmen
were lost. And, more than six-hundred bombers
suffered battle damage. The stats on the 92nd alone*

were, <u>one</u> aircraft lost and <u>twenty-six</u> badly damaged.
Only thirty-six went up. <u>Nine</u> crewmen were MIA and
<u>five</u> were wounded.]

The success of the ME-262 was astonishing. We had no crystal balls, and to the airmen who had to carry on in the face of such odds, the future was certainly foreboding. Had Hitler used this weapon in the manner his experts wanted to, I shudder to think of the consequences.

⌘

Losses like those on March 18th, were not the only tragedies we endured. Watching comrades go down, bail out or suffer from injuries, was bad enough. But, also disconcerting, was finding a comrade hanging by his neck in the latrine, or slumped on the floor with his brains splattered on the urinals with his .45in one hand. During my stay at Podington, I personally knew of several suicides.

How many men committed suicide in the 8th during the war will probably never be known. In analyzing this phenomenon with other so-called barracks psychologists, we all seemed to agree that these men shared certain characteristics. Most seemed to be loners. They spent many long hours lying on their bunks staring at nothing but space while most everyone else sought out other endeavors. To keep our mind off our business, among other things, we could be found drinking beer at the Enlisted Men's Club, or drinking warm mild and bitters and playing darts in a local pub. And then, of course, most important, in my case, there was Annie.

18

ANNIE WAS OUT OF TOWN ON MARCH 19, VISITING RELATIVES. I had some time off and went to London with friends. We were minding our own business drinking beer, when suddenly the doors flew open and in stomped four American paratroopers. Once inside the door they planted their boots, stuck out their chests and with hands on their hips arrogantly shouted out an obscenity involving the Queen of England. Now, there were a lot of things they could have said to provoke a fight, but this was the very worst. I truly consider myself fortunate that we were able to duck under a table, and like the cowards we were, crawl to the back door, while the bottles, chairs and glasses, went flying indiscriminately around the room.

The next morning, before catching a cab to the St. Pancras Station, I stopped at a jewelry store and purchased a ring. It was my intention to make an honest man of myself and ask Annie to marry me. Arriving at the station early, I bought a cup of tea and sat down at the same table as a distinguished looking gentleman. The man was impeccably dressed, and carried an attache case. He struck up a conversation and then lectured me on the evils of the British people. He told me of how they had persecuted the Irish for hundreds of years. As it turned out, he was an Irish diplomat from Dublin. Since Ireland was neutral, he said, he had little opportunity to talk to Americans.

Being a nineteen-year-old American risking my life almost every day so he could enjoy his freedom, and knowing that the British had, in all probability, saved us all from defeat, and, carrying a ring in my pocket intended for one of those British subjects he was berating, let it be said that I did not take kindly to his lecture.

Thursday, March 22.
Mission number twenty-three: Bottrop

George Patton was about to cross the Rhine. Our job today was to drop one hundred pound anti personnel bombs behind the German lines on the military barracks at *Bottrop*. This town was about twenty miles east of the Belgium border. We would go in at low level for improved accuracy. We did *not* want to hit our own troops. The 325th was leading the group, so we were flying Deputy Lead. Lt. Bekker's VIP for this mission was our Operations Officer. This mission was marred due to a mechanical failure in Bekker's aircraft, some of our bombs tragically landed on the wrong side of the lines... the last thing we wanted to happen. However, the Low and High squadrons were on target and Patton did cross the Rhine that day.

Saturday, March 24.
Mission number twenty-four: Hesepe

The people in High Wycombe [8th Air Force Headquarters] must have been concerned with the large number of losses incurred on March 18, for today we were going all out after ME-262 bases. In fact, for the first time since I had been here, the 92nd was putting *all* four squadrons in the air. Three squadrons, the 326th, 327th, and 407th bombed a base at *Achmer* with the 40th "C" Force, while we led the 325th to a base at *Hesepe* with the 40th "D" Force. Both targets were destroyed.

⌘

Lt. Bekker's radio operator had completed his tour of duty two missions before the rest of his crew, on March 22. On Sunday, March 25, I was notified that I would replace him as the new Group Lead ROMG. I could have refused, some men turned it down because Group Lead's only flew every fourth mission, and they didn't like sweating out the free time in between. They wanted to get it over with and go back to the States as soon as possible. To help compensate for this, lead crews only had to fly thirty missions… and I liked that. Besides, I didn't sweat out the days in between. I spent most of them with Annie. The fact that the Group Lead aircraft was the primary target for German anti aircraft batteries and fighters, did not thrill me, but I think the fact that I had flown in so many "Tail End Charlie's" and "Purple Heart Corners," made it easier for me.

To be honest, perhaps the most important thing that prompted me to accept the job was my ego. Group Lead crews were considered the best. The respect and perks that came with the job appealed to me. Flying Squadron Lead had done great things for my self esteem. I had gained a lot of confidence and I seemed to have come to terms with my fear. By now I had learned that every normal person flew combat with fear, but some did a better job of putting that fear aside than others. And like most men, I believe my fear was partly smothered by pride. That's why in the earlier days, even when I was desperately trying to think of a way out, I always showed up and did my job. Another benefit of flying Group Lead, besides flying with the very best, was the fact that I now had company in the radio room. Lt. Richard Kendall, another Michigander, was our radar navigator, or, 'Mickey' man.

Friday, March 30.
Mission number twenty-five: Bremen

Today we would lead thirty-six aircraft to strike a bridge over the Weser River near Bremen. As we gathered around the nose of the only H2X aircraft on the base, I was officially introduced to the Commanding Officer of the 92nd Bomb Group, Colonel James Wilson. He was in his flying clothes and would be our VIP on this mission. I'm not sure he remembered that rainy night in February when he gave me a lift.

Now, Flying Group Lead, we were the *first* to take off. Everyone assembled on us. It was my duty now, to encode and send the two check point messages on the way to the target, a bomb strike message, and two check point messages on the way home. I was the *only* man in the group who could break radio silence on CW outside of an emergency.

The mission was carried off without a glitch. We destroyed the bridge and returned safely to Podington.

19

Saturday, March 31.
Annie's

SATURDAY, MARCH 31, WAS THE FIRST DAY OF A THREE DAY PASS I SPENT WITH ANNIE AFTER THE BREMEN MISSION. Annie's mother had gone to London to be with her husband at a dinner being held in his honor. For what, I never did know. She would be home late Sunday afternoon. Annie's father would stay in London. Accept for Charley and Fanny, we had the whole place to ourselves.

We did all the usual stuff with the horses. With Charley's help I was getting pretty good now. It was getting a little warmer these days and the leaves and blossoms were breaking out all over. Our hikes through the woods were nothing short of spectacular. Afterwards, we spent time relaxing by her pond.

On Sunday, Annie packed a lunch and we took a short ride to a hilltop and watched the 92nd return from a mission. She said this was the first time she'd been here since the Battle of Britain. People used to gather here and watch the dog fights. After her brother was killed, she just couldn't come back.

On my last evening there we went to the Cinema and saw Judy Garland in "Meet Me in St. Louis."Then we met Annie's mother at the pub and shared a drink or two with some of her friends and neighbors.

On April 4th, over Fassberg, the group lost another crew in the 327th. The crew of pilot Tony Marozas. I knew every man on that crew. It was that squadron's sixth loss in less than thirty days. *Half* of the squadron. In that period of time the 327th lost more aircraft than the other three squadrons put together.

Tom Shanahan put down his pen, struck a match and relit his pipe. As he puffed, he looked over at my sketch. I would say that if I had a talent for anything in this life, it was art. We were in the day room and I was just finishing a sketch of Tom as he wrote home. [I still have that sketch.]

"You're pretty good," he said, "you should go to art school when you get home." We had not led the group that day, so it was one of my days off. But not for Tom, he had seen nine of his compatriots go down that afternoon. One of them, Anthony Marozos, was his copilot at Ardmore. Anthony, better known as Tony, had become a Pilot, acquiring his own crew over a month ago. I'm sure this loss is what prompted Tom to broach a subject that we had never discussed before.

"You mean, *If* I get home, ke-mo-sa-be," I said.

"Do me a favor," Tom went on, "If I don't make it... go see my parents." I put down my pencil and looked up. He was serious. I couldn't blame him. Half of his squadron were rookies. Only seven crews had been here more than thirty days. The 327th had had an unprecedented streak of bad luck.

"Only if you do the same for me... but don't worry, things are bound to get better," I replied

How wrong I was.

Thursday, April 5.
Mission number twenty-six: Ingolstadt

On the Blue Danube, somewhat north of Munich, in Bavaria, is the city of *Ingolstadt.* The Germans had an ordinance depot at Ingolstadt, supplying arms to their troops in Czechoslovakia. And on April 5, we were going to put a stop to that by destroying that depot.

It was a *twenty-seven-eighty,* and my last mission with Peter O. Bekker's crew. With the exception of Kendall and me, everyone was finishing their tour today. Lt. Bekker was now Captain Bekker. He had just received a well-deserved promotion. Lt. Col. Cox was our VIP and would lead the group.

Thirty-six aircraft took off for this mission. Only thirty reached the target. One aircraft, in the 407th, was delayed in taking off. While trying to catch up, much the same as Hank had once done, they were attacked by an ME-262 jet fighter. They sustained heavy damage but were able to jettison their bombs and return safely to Podington. For various other reasons five other aircraft aborted and returned to the base.

My bomb strike message to Podington reported excellent results and we led the thirty remaining aircraft home without further incident.

20

WHEN I CALLED ANNIE THAT NIGHT SHE SAID THAT HER FATHER WAS HOME AND THEY WERE IN THE MIDDLE OF A DISCUSSION ABOUT OUR ENGAGEMENT. She said that she couldn't talk now, but she would tell me all about it tomorrow. [We were supposed to meet for lunch the next day at our favorite pub.]

I knew that she was dreading this confrontation with her father when he found out that she was engaged. Her mother had warned her to be prepared for it. Needless to say, I was on pins and needles until we met the next day.

I was early and had two bottles of stout to fortify myself. When she arrived, we moved to a quiet table in a corner where we could talk. I can't recall all the details, but it went something like this: She said her father scoffed at our getting married. He could understand her having a love affair, but was sure it was only 'puppy love.' We were too young to get married. He would never permit it. Then her mother stepped in. She said her father's timing was terrible. She thought we should wait and discuss this when my tour was over. In the end, her father dismissed the subject, agreeing to talk about it later.

Since I never believed I was going to get out of this alive anyway, I thought there was no harm done. So why worry about it now. If I made it, we could deal with her father then.

Tuesday, April 10.
Mission number twenty-seven: Oranienburg

One-thousand-two-hundred-eighty bombers would participate in another major strike at ME-262 air bases and manufacturing plants today. There was no doubt about who held the supremacy of the air now, but this jet could inflict enormous damage on us and make us pay dearly to maintain that advantage. We hoped that this mission would be the fatal blow to the troublesome aircraft.

1st Lt. Thomas White was our new Group Lead pilot replacing Bekker, and I would fly this mission as his ROMG. George Jaeger was back with me as engineer and Richard Kendall was our "Mickey" man. We would lead the group today on another *twenty-seven-eighty.* Our target was an ME-262 base at Oranienburg, a suburb of Berlin. Our VIP on this mission would be our Operations Officer.

Before the day was over, we saw spectacular dog fights. Our screen of Mustangs downed *twenty* of the superior ME-262s. This was due partly to a shortage of experienced German pilots, pilots lost in Hitler's ill advised attack in the Ardennes, but it was also due to the skill of our 'little friends.' However, the jets *still*

knocked down *ten* B-17s. The losses were in the 95th, 100th and 390th Bomb Groups. Trading *twenty* of their fighters and fighter pilots for *ten* of our B-17s and *ninety* of our well-trained crewmen was rather one sided. Simply put though, we could afford it and they could not.

I was not scheduled to fly on Wednesday, April 11, because we were not leading the group. But unless we were on leave, we were required to attend all briefing sessions, only after the last plane took off were we free to go.

During the long wait for thirty-six planes to take off, I leaned my chair back against an outside wall and was trying to catch a nap. Half awake, I could hear the familiar sound of the Fortresses as, one by one, they ran their engines up and rumbled off heading toward assembly.

Suddenly, I was pitched forward, and arms outstretched, I slid on the floor like a modern baseball player sliding into second base. As I slid, I heard the delayed KABOOM. No one had to tell me what happened, I already knew. Leaping to my feet, I rushed to the door. Outside, in the early morning haze everyone was running toward the mushrooming cloud at the end of the runway.

Fire trucks and ambulances raced past me and were at the scene as I arrived. I recognized the crewmen medics were hustling into ambulances. It was a crew in the 326th. Miraculously, everyone escaped with no major injuries. They had blown a tire just before lift off and somehow had managed to get airborne. They got the landing gear up but hit the prop-wash from the plane ahead, then hit the trees.

Thursday, April 12

President Roosevelt died in Warm Springs, Georgia, and Harry S. Truman was sworn in as the new president of the United States today.

Friday, April 13

Allied troops entered the Buchenwald and Belsen death camps exposing to the world the full horror of the atrocities committed there.

Back in the States, on Friday, April 13, brother Wayne boarded a train bound for Fort Sheridan, Illinois. He was assigned to seat number 13. As he later went through the line for his physical, his hand was stamped #13. Wayne went on to serve in the 11th Airborne, making five successful jumps. Evidently his lucky number was 'thirteen.'

Patton was moving so fast now, at times the 9th Air Force [fighters] were sent out to find him. We would be briefed for a mission, and went as far as revving up our engines, only to have red flares fired from the tower scrubbing the mission. Patton was slowly taking our targets away from us.

Saturday, April 14

On Saturday, April 14, like a bolt of lightning, something completely unexpected happened. Looking back on it now, for me, I believe it was a life changing event. George Jaeger and I received orders to report to the USAAF rest center in Nice, France for a two week, what was called, a 'flak' leave. We were told to prepare for a flight to the Riviera in the morning. This was *very* good news for us, and possibly could have saved our lives. It meant no missions for two weeks with the war winding down fast. I called Annie with the good news so she wouldn't worry. [I wouldn't be able to call her from France.] Then I started packing.

Sunday, April 15.
Nice, France

I knew of no one that had been to this rest center. In fact, I wasn't aware that it existed. The accommodations were fantastic. The food was like nothing we had ever experienced before. The area was absolutely beautiful. I had never seen so many flowers and palm trees. The beaches were full of round smooth stones, but that didn't bother us, we had no swim suits so it didn't matter. We did roll up our pants and did some wading, but the rocks were slippery and the water was cold. As Jaeger and I played ping pong on the lawn, roamed the beaches and took in the sights of the Riviera for the next two weeks, major events were happening around us and back at Podington.

Monday, April 16

Canadian troops captured Arnhem, in Holland. And the U.S. 7th Army arrived at the outskirts of Nuremberg.

Wednesday, April 18

Today the concentration camp at Dachau was liberated.

Thursday, April 19

German units began to surrender in the Ruhr, and Patton entered Czechoslovakia.

Friday, April 20

On Hitler's 56th birthday today, the Allies took Nuremberg, and Stuttgart.

Saturday, April 21

Russian General Zhukov entered the suburbs of Berlin.

Sunday, April 22

The U.S. 7th Army crossed the Elbe.

Monday, April 23

As Hitler was besieged in his bunker in Berlin, Goering offered to take over and run the war for him. Hitler was furious and ordered Goering arrested. The order was never carried out.

Tuesday, April 24

Today Berlin was completely surrounded.

Wednesday, April 25

An unusual conference was held in San Francisco today. Its purpose was to draw up the Constitution of the United Nations.

Thursday, April 26

Patton entered Austria, and the U.S. 1st Army reached Lake Constance.

Friday, April 27

The Soviets took Templehof Airport in Berlin and the Allies demanded an *unconditional* surrender of all German armies.

Saturday, April 28, 1945

As I returned to Podington, Mussolini and his mistress, Clara Petacci, were apprehended by Italian partisans as they attempted to escape to Switzerland. They were both shot and hung up by their ankles in the main square in Milan. The Soviets were within one mile of Hitler's bunker. And the Allies were advancing on Munich.

Back at Podington I was stunned to hear that Tom Shanahan had gone down on a mission to Dresden on April 17. While doing a three-sixty over Dresden, the 92nd unexpectedly found themselves on a collision course over the target area with another group, and five planes went down. Two from the 92nd, and three from the other group. The two from the 92nd were from the 327th, and one of them was Tom's.

Ironically, two missions after Tom went down, Group Leader, Lt. Thomas White, of the 325th, led the 92nd to Pilson on April 25th, on the groups last mission. In all probability, had I not been in France, I would have been his radio operator on that last mission. One plane went down that day and… it was from the 327th.

When I learned that my friend Tom went down I was devastated. We had shared so much. Circumstances had created a bond between us that no friendship could ever equal. He was like a brother to me. And now he was gone. But there was hope, three chutes had been sighted.

Sunday, April 29

Hitler married Eva Braun and appointed Admiral Doenitz to succeed him. He accused the German people of failing him in his struggle against Bolshevism.

Monday, April 30

Hitler and Eva Braun committed suicide. Their bodies were doused with gasoline and burned outside their bunker as the Russians were advancing toward the Reichstag.

Tuesday, May 1

In a radio broadcast from Hamburg, Admiral Doenitz told the world that Hitler was dead. He did not mention that he had committed suicide. He went on to say that it was now his duty [Doenitz's] to save the German people from Bolshevism.

That same day Reichsfuerher Joseph Goebbels died, along with his wife and six children. The children were poisoned by their mother. Two SS guards carried out the Reichsfuerher's last request and shot him and his wife. Their bodies were then burned in the same manner and place as Hitler's.

Saturday, May 5

Lt. Hammond, of the 326th, crashed and burned while on a routine practice flight. His radio operator was the only survivor.

Monday, May 7

Generaladmiral Hans Georg von Friedeburg and Generaloberst Alfred Jodl, representing Germany, signed an unconditional surrender at General Eisenhower's headquarters. The war with Germany would officially end at 2301 hours on Tuesday, May 8, 1945. The allies then proclaimed May 8, VE [Victory in Europe] Day.

Tuesday, May 8

Colonel Wilson, speaking from the boxing ring on our athletic field at Podington, gave us the official news and said that we were restricted to the base, by order of General Eisenhower.

There were no celebrations at Podington that day. Almost to a man, I believe, Eisenhower's order was deeply resented. We were told that he felt this action was necessary to prevent disputes with our Allies over 'who won the war.' As a result, we felt left out. And on top of all that, I was dying to celebrate this day with Annie.

We silently listened to all the celebrations being broadcast from capitals around the world. Giant ticker tape parades were taking place in New York. Everywhere in the U. S., Stateside GI's were dancing in the streets. Most of whom, we knew, had never seen combat. [Statistics of World War II show that only one out of ten servicemen *ever* saw combat.]

Perhaps Eisenhower's order was a wise one, but to young men who had been through so much to bring this day about it seemed like a hollow victory at the time. I can easily find some parallels with my emotions then and the emotions of our Vietnam veterans many years later.

The real irony was, that as celebrations continued in the States, young Americans were still dying in Europe. Small pockets of Germans still fought on.

Friday, May 11

The last remnants of the German army in Czechoslovakia surrendered on May 11. But in the Pacific, fierce fighting was reported on Okinawa, as the U.S. was preparing for the greatest invasion of all time, the invasion of Japan. Both sides were expecting enormous casualties, for the Japanese were vowing to fight to the last man.

⌘

It was about this time that some of our compatriots interned in Sweden, or Switzerland, started to trickle back, as well as POWs from Germany. I personally talked to some of them. One being my ex-bombardier, Ted Fossberg who had been interned in Sweden with Lt. Ringsred.

Those from Sweden said that they had been treated very well, better than the Germans. One reason for that was that our men were there by accident in the line of duty. The Germans were there because they were deserters. However, Switzerland was another story. Our guys back from Switzerland said that the Germans there were treated better than they were. The Swiss, they thought, were more sympathetic to the German cause than that of the Allies.

Then I heard that Tom's tail gunner had just arrived on the base. I had new hope for my friend. I immediately looked the man up. He said that the tail section broke away from the aircraft and started to float down like a leaf, he simply snapped his chute on, jumped, and pulled the rip cord. It happened so fast, he said, if Tom was not wearing his chute, he was SOL.

[For a long time I was tormented by what I had heard. I knew I would not have had my chute on. The thought of my friend out there with no chute triggered my old dream and sometimes to this day it comes back to haunt me. A grim reminder of the past that will probably follow me to the grave.]

Back in 1945 however, my conscious mind chose to believe that Tom had survived and would turn up in some German prison camp, after all, three chutes had been sighted. It was the best way I had of dealing with my feelings at the time.

I also remember visiting an officer with a cast on his leg from his hip to his toes, in fact, I remember signing it. For many years I had been suffering under the illusion that this officer was John Paul, Tom's pilot. But, in a telephone conversation with John Paul in 1994, I learned that I was wrong. But that's another story. [See epilogue.]

As I recall, this officer, the one with the leg in a cast, said that one minute he was flying along and the next thing he remembered he was in mid air. He recalled looking back and seeing his plane blow up. He was wearing a back pack chute, pulled the ripcord and broke his leg landing.

Tuesday, May 15

One week after VE Day, I was no longer a teenager. Tuesday, May 15, 1945 was my twentieth birthday. It was on my birthday that I learned that Annie's father had come home for good. Things were happening so fast, and were so hectic in those days, that I rarely got to see, or even talk to Annie.

21

RUMORS WERE RAMPANT THEN REGARDING OUR FUTURE. In bits and pieces we learned what was in store for us. A point system was established based on length of service, number of days overseas, number of combat hours flown, etc. All personnel of the 92nd were put in one pool. The 326th and 407th squadrons would be disbanded. The 325th and 327th would be reorganized using personnel from all four squadrons. The 325th was going to France, the 327th to Africa. Both squadrons would participate in an undertaking to be called *The Green Project.* High point pilots, copilots, navigators, engineers, radio operators, and ground personnel required to support them, would be assigned to this project. Low point pilots, copilots, engineers, and *all* gunners, bombardiers, and personnel not required to support the 325th and 327th would return to the States for reassignment. The newest and best B-17s in the group would be stripped down and modified to carry passengers. Benches would be installed in the waist and bomb bays. Most remaining Flying Fortresses would be destroyed.

I was surprised to learn that I was going with the 325th to France. I felt sure that I would go back to the States and end up with some cushy training job until the war in the Pacific ended. Then go to school… send for Annie… and live happily ever after.

How naive I was.

[Looking back over my life I can't count the times an unexpected bounce of the ball has profoundly changed it. At this particular time the ball was bouncing in so many different directions that it made my head spin. It started with that trip to the Riviera. Then Tom Shanahan went down, and the war suddenly ended. Being restricted to the base didn't help, and now we were flying on some kind of special mission almost every day. And on top of all that, I would be going to France soon, for God only knew how long.

My educated guess is that, about 80% of the men in the 8th Air Force went back to the US shortly after the war ended. Part of those remaining, the 92nd's 325th and 327th, went to France and Africa to participate in the event called The Green Project.

Although thousands upon thousands of men came home from Europe via this project, and hundreds of French Jews were returned to their homeland because of it, to this day, besides those I know who are still alive that participated in it, I have never met anyone whoever heard of it. Furthermore, I have yet to find it mentioned in any book, or, in any documentary. What a shame. We spent almost seven months of our lives, at some sacrifice I must say, on a project, that few people ever heard of.]

We were only five man crew's now. I was assigned to the crew of pilot Lt. J. W. Cooper. We called him JW, I never did know his first name, I guess he wanted it that way. JW was a likeable, fun-loving guy, very handsome, and a ladies man. Lt. Bob Juenger was our copilot and second in command. Lt. Joe Diamond was our navigator. The only evidence of Joe's wound from the March 9th mission to Kassel was a scar on his forehead. Our engineer was my old friend, George Jaeger.

⌘

Since VE Day, we were going for weeks on end with no time off. We were in the air almost daily. Among other things, we flew US army ground personnel on 1,000 foot low level sightseeing tours of the battle fields and ruins of Europe's once great cities. Then, while preparations were being made for the move to France, we became an airline service. We flew VIPs to places like Belfast, Edinburgh, and the Rock of Gibralter, just to name a few. The good part was, we usually RONd [remained overnight] with them, and flew them back the next day. We never knew why they were going where they went. As far as I know, they never talked to anyone but JW, and I figured that he was just following orders.

⌘

One day I had a close call with a bull. Can you imagine surviving the war, only to get killed by a bull? Remember that bull I saw the day I arrived at Podington? Well, he was penned up in a field about one-hundred yards long and fifty yards wide. The trouble was, that field was between my barracks and the mess hall and one day I got tired of walking around it. When I saw the bull on the far side of the pen, I decided to take a short cut and save about two hundred yards. I've got to tell you, that bull was the biggest, meanest bull you ever saw, and when he saw me invade his territory he became *very* upset. I was over half way across the field when I felt the ground tremble under my feet. I never ran so fast in all my life. The ground sounded like thunder as he bore down on me. He pulled up short with a snort as I leaped to the other side of the fence just in time. It took the rest of the walk to the mess hall to regain my composure and stop trembling.

Wednesday, May 23

Reichsfuerher Heinrich Himmler was captured by the British. He committed suicide by putting a cyanide capsule in his mouth and breaking it with his teeth.

Tuesday, May 29

The first convoy of equipment and ground personnel left Podington bound for France today. Jeeps, trucks and trailers from the 325th started for Southampton. They would cross the channel on LCTs and land in Le Havre, France. From Le Havre the convoy would travel a little more than 700 miles to a small town called, Istres.

   With mixed feelings I said goodbye to ex crew members, barracks mates, and other comrades going back to the States. Although I would miss them, at that time I certainly did not envy them. I was told that they were going to be retrained in B-29s and would participate in the invasion of Japan.

⌘

I really liked JW, but soon found that he had a penchant for buzzing. Buzzing clouds wasn't so bad. It was like riding a roller coaster. There were times though that I feared the wings would fall off. But what really bothered me was the way he buzzed the English countryside.

J W. Cooper 1945

One day I was sitting in the nose with Joe when he buzzed an English Manor. We were heading straight for the second floor of the main house just a few feet over the well-manicured lawn. If there was anyone in that house watching, we must have scared the daylights out of them. In the last second before impact, he pulled that Fort up and we roared over the roof top. Then, just like playing leapfrog, he came back down just above the flower beds and was heading toward a grove of trees. Just before we hit the grove he banked and slipped the tip of our left wing through an opening in the trees. I swear our wingtip almost brushed the grass as we sailed by those trees.

I looked at Joe and wondered if I were as pale as he. *Every* bulletin board on the base contained a picture of the remains of a B-17 scattered all over the English countryside bearing the message, BUZZING IS STRICTLY FORBIDDEN. Back at the hardstand, after we jumped from the nose hatch, I told Joe that this guy was crazy; that he should have been a fighter pilot. My only ambition now was to get home safely. I had come too far to wind up splattered all over the English countryside. I told Joe that I was going to ask for a transfer to another crew. About an hour later I was surprised when JW walked into my barracks and asked if there was somewhere we could talk. We went to my room and closed the door. Joe had talked to him about buzzing and told him how I felt, he said. He wanted me to know that it wouldn't happen again and he hoped that I would stay on.

Under those conditions I agreed to stay on and added that he probably should have been a fighter pilot. He smiled and said that he always wanted to be a fighter pilot, but the army had a penchant for putting a square peg in a round hole. We shook hands and he left. As it turned out this would become the closest knit crew I ever had the pleasure of flying with. We went on to have many good times together in England, Ireland, Scotland, France, Italy, Gibraltar, Africa and even Germany.

Monday, June 4

This Monday the crew spent the day supervising and helping to load our aircraft with equipment bound for France. The weight had to be properly distributed and the load tightly secured so it could not shift. In the morning we were going to make our first trip to our new base in France.

Tuesday, June 5

Marseilles is a large seaport on the Mediterranean Sea. Just east of Marseilles, along the coast, is the French Riviera, playground of the rich and famous. On this shore you will find Cannes, Antibes, Nice, Monaco, Monte Carlo and the beautiful Maritime Alps. Not far north of Marseilles is a small town called Istres. Further north, is the ancient town of Avignon. But when people describe the beauty of southern France, they ignore La Crau, the desert-like wasteland surrounding Istres. Nothing but a plain of rocks and sand, La Crau is swept by fierce northerly winds called, The Mistral. These winds blow on an average of 110 days a year. When men of the 92nd referred to Istres, they used a very uncomplimentary term. They called it 'the Ass Hole of the World.'

Looking over our new home on Tuesday, June 5, was most disheartening. At one time this airfield had been a French experimental aircraft station. They had constructed buildings of concrete, with tree-lined paved streets that gave them some protection from The Mistral. We soon found that fine brown sand penetrated everything. There was no escaping it.

The Germans had used this field for a fighter base. When they left, in 1944, they destroyed it. They poured cement down the sewage drains and booby trapped and mined the whole area. When we arrived that day. engineers were drilling for water and had started to clear the area of land mines and booby traps. The only safe places to walk were narrow roped off paths. Helping in all this were 1,500 German SS PWs, guarded by our MPs.

As we explored the base, I ran into an acquaintance who had come over in the advance party. He told me that all of Europe was in the grips of a severe food shortage. The war had destroyed many farms and consumed vital fuel needed to run them. Most farmers in occupied territories had fled to the hills and mountains during the war, choosing to engage in guerrilla warfare rather than be conscripted into German forced labor camps.

The farm animal and poultry population had been devastated by the war; accidentally killed or consumed by foraging armies. My friend said that he was trading candy bars and cigarettes for champagne and wine. And since there was a severe shortage of drinking water, until the wells were in, he was drinking a lot of champagne and wine. As we toured the base, we saw PWs constructing prefabricated buildings for our mess hall and headquarters, while others were pitching tents for our temporary quarters... later we would move into prefabricated barracks.

Sunday, June 10. Annie

I said goodby to Annie on June 10th. We never did have that talk with her father. It's probably a good thing, since the war was over and I had no more missions to fly. Tuesday we were leaving Podington for the last time. As for our engagement? Everything was put on hold until the war in Japan was over. Although I didn't know it at the time, this would be the last time I would ever see my first love.

Tuesday, June 12

On Tuesday, June 12, 1945, we lumbered down the runway at Podington for the last time. Again, the plane was loaded down with equipment for our new home. All of my worldly possessions were on board in my duffle bag. A few hours later we landed at our new home in France. We spent the first few days getting organized and learning more about our role in the Green Project.

Our primary job would be to ferry high point infantrymen to Casablanca, North Africa. Most of these men would be from Patton's 3rd Army. In Casablanca, we would only be on the ground long enough to unload our human cargo, then we would make a short trip to Port Lyautey. In Port Lyautey, we would spend the night with our friends in the 327th, who were now billeted there.

It was the job of the 327th to fly our cargo from Casablanca to the Azores. The ATC [Air Transport Command] would take it from there and fly them to the States. Our secondary job was to return French DPs [displaced persons] now in Africa, to their home

country, France. These people were French Jews who
fled to Africa to escape the German death camps.

As I mentioned before, in 1945 commercial air
travel was in its infancy and today most people take this
mode of travel for granted. But even today many people
suffer from aero phobia [the fear of flying]. One notable
man that eventually conquered this phobia was the late
President Lyndon B. Johnson.

I understand that the late newspaper columnist Mike
Royko had the same problem, as well as the renown
sportscaster and ex-NFL coach John Madden. In 1945
this fear was even more prevalent than it is today and
we would find this phobia even among these battle
hardened infantrymen. They all wanted to go home and
as quickly as possible, but when it got right down to
actually boarding an airplane, *that* was a different story.

Friday, June 15.
Istres, France

At the crack of dawn, we, and two other air crews,
gathered around a Red Cross canteen truck parked in
front of three modified B-17Gs. We were waiting for the
arrival of ninety-six high point infantrymen from the 3rd
Army. These three crews had been selected to kick off
the *Green Project*. The most unusual air lift of its time.

We playfully joked with the Red Cross girls who
were passing out coffee in the chill, crisp, morning
air. All eyes turned to the east as we heard the rumble
of engines caused by a small caravan of GI personnel
carriers as they arrived at the main gate in the distance.

Once through the gate the caravan turned in our
direction. As they approached, they created billows of
grey dust, marring a rose, peach and purple horizon. In

a matter of minutes their wheels ground to a halt as they came to a stop nearby.

After hot coffee and donuts the men were directed to their respective aircraft. JW delivered a short prepared speech to the group of men we would transport that day, and presented each man with a wallet size card.

I still have one of those cards. One side of the card says:

THIS IS TO CERTIFY THAT.... (The man's name)...... having defeated the Axis powers in Europe, has been flown from France to Africa on the first leg of the journey home in a Flying Fortress of the 92nd Bombardment group---**Fame's Favored Few**---the oldest bomber group in Europe. He is now a member of the

92nd GROUP SHORT SNORTER CLUB
Duration of flight............... . . hours

Date............... . . 1945. Pilot............... . .
(JW would fill in the blank spaces and sign the card.)

On the other side of the card was a map with an explanation, it said:

The route flown starts from Istres airfield on the Rhone delta near Marseilles. The coast of Spain is followed to Gibraltar, thence along the Atlantic North African coast to Casablanca. The trip, almost 1,000 miles over water, is flown in approximately 5 ½ hours.

Next we helped the men put on parachute harnesses, hooked up their chest pack chutes, and gave them instructions on how to bail out. Until now, these men had not contemplated the possibility of bailing out. The very thought of bailing out created extreme anxiety in some, and downright terror in others. They began to gripe and grumble, making remarks like, "If I wanted to fly, I would have joined the Air Corps!" Or, "I didn't walk all across Europe with Krauts shooting at me, only to wind up getting killed in a God damned air-o-plane!" One man actually stopped at the waist door and refused to board. We were at a stalemate until an infantry captain came over and gave him a direct order to board.

Needless to say, we were not prepared for this reaction, and future boardings went more smoothly with experience. We learned to be more casual, putting our passengers at ease by smiling a lot and joking with them. We played down the chutes as, 'just another stupid army regulation.' They could relate to that. A little bragging about how many missions we had flown without *ever* bailing out, didn't seem to hurt either.

Our plea to our superiors to make an exception to this process fell on deaf ears. The returning DPs were not required to wear chutes, we argued. But the decision makers must have thought that the return trip was safer... Right!

One thing I learned on the very first trip: *Never* say anything derogatory about the 3rd Army's highly controversial General Patton. These enlisted men fondly called him 'Old Blood and Guts.' I was lucky to find this out before I said anything. I had been under the impression that Patton was disliked by the enlisted man. And I later learned that he at one time *was*. He had earned a bad reputation with the enlisted men in the campaigns in Africa and Sicily. But then, after a slapping incident in an army hospital, he lost his command and sat out 'D' day in England. He completely reversed his image when he was later given command of the 3rd

Army in Europe. One private related the following story that first day:

"We were held up at this river when Old Blood and Guts pulled up in his jeep. He asked us what the hell the hold up was. We told him, machine gun fire on the other side of the river, Sir. At that Patton didn't say a word, he just got out of the jeep, took off his gun belt containing two ivory handled pistols, jumped in the river, swam to the other side and back, climbed out soaking wet and shouted, *"'Now get the hell across this fucking river!'"* I had heard some tall stories before, but the knowing smiles and affirmative nods of his buddies made me believe the man was telling the truth.

At 0700 hours we took off and headed out over the Mediterranean Sea with a plane load of infantrymen for the first historic flight of *The Green Project.* Five hours and twenty minutes later JW was banking over Casablanca and I saw this large sprawling city for the first time.

I had never seen a city like this before. Most of the buildings were white with red tiled roofs, and the streets were lined with Palm trees. I had seen the movie *Casablanca* and was a little awed looking down on that world renown Moroccan city of mystery and intrigue. Being a twenty-year-old romantic, I visualized a black piano player singing *As Time Goes By*. A misty eyed Ingrid Bergman bidding farewell to Humphrey Bogart. And then Claude Rains and Bogart walking on a wet runway and disappearing into the fog at what was supposed to be this same airport.

The screech of tires as the plane landed brought me back to reality. And now these infantry men were all smiles. The first leg of their journey was behind them and they were still alive. And they did it without having to bail out. The crew never left the aircraft. After the last passenger had disembarked, we turned around and took off again. Thirty minutes later we were in Port Lyautey.

We found Port Lyautey [or Kenitra, now] on the edge of the Sahara Desert, on the mouth of the Sebou River. It is a large port on the North Atlantic Ocean. We would make many such trips in the coming months, always arriving in the early afternoon, which gave us plenty of time for sightseeing. The French Quarter in Port Lyautey was very nice, just like an oasis in the desert. But the Arab section, which surrounded the French Quarter on three sides [the ocean being on the fourth], appalled and sickened me.

I had never seen such miserable living conditions. Most Arabs lived in makeshift shelters constructed of any piece of junk they could find. Odd shapes of sheet metal, cardboard and chicken wire. Anything. There were no plumbing or sanitation facilities. The desert was their bathroom. Both males and females wore robes. The women wore veils. When mother nature called they simply walked a few yards out on the desert and squatted. The perimeter of their village was dotted with human waste and flies.

Flies were everywhere. There was no escaping them. The small children wore no clothes. Their heads were shaved except for a small tassel on the top. Many had open sores, covered with flies. Since it was useless to brush the flies off, they simply ignored them.

And the children followed us everywhere, begging for 'bonbons.' I saw a makeshift meat market, nothing but a shanty. Hanging from racks in this shanty were skinned cats, dogs and large rodents. All were black with flies. An old woman sat cross legged on the desert floor selling some kind of dried fruit. The fruit too, was covered with flies.

We were warned to *never* travel alone in Port Lyautey, and to completely avoid certain parts of the city. The Arabs hated the French and the Americans were friends of the French, thus the Arabs hated the Americans. In fact, while traveling through the Arab section in a personnel carrier one day, we were chased by Arab children throwing stones at the truck.

The Arabs provided all the menial labor for the French. Hundreds of Arabs would move a railroad freight car from one siding to another, *by hand*. They also did the same thing for the Air force, working in the mess hall and cleaning the latrines. One of our men caught an Arab laborer stealing a pack of Lucky Strike cigarettes from his duffle bag. He reported the man to our MPs. They, in turn, gave him to the French Gendarmes. The French ruled with an iron fist and took the man outside the main gate, then beat him senseless. When the man who turned him in protested, he was told that the beating was necessary, the only way to keep these people in line.

In the morning about two dozen French DPs of both sexes boarded our aircraft. They were the first group to return to their homeland since the war ended, just thirty-seven days ago.

Although the war was over in Europe, Americans were still fighting in the Pacific. Just recently, General Buckner was killed in the fighting on Okinawa. Our navy was bombing Wake Island, while 30,000 Australians had just landed on Borneo. In England, Lord Haw Haw had been found guilty of treason and had been executed.

22

WHEN WE WERE NOT FLYING GREEN PROJECT RUNS, WE FLEW LIBERTY RUNS TO ROME OR PARIS. It was almost like a private airline. All personnel with a 48-hour pass or more, could select either one of these great cities to visit. And when air crews flew Liberty runs they RONd.

I fell in love with Rome on my first visit. The women were beautiful. I was surprised by the number of blonds and redheads in that city. In my mind I had wrongly stereotyped Italians, I had expected all Italians to have olive complections and dark black hair.

The wonderful climate in Rome, unlike London, produces beautifully tanned bodies, enabling women to expose them to their best advantage. At a time when nylons were almost impossible to come by, for example, they didn't need them. Fresh, bright colored, or white, summer garments were worn year round.

I visited the Piazza Venezia, and stood on the balcony that Mussolini made famous. This was the spot where the arrogant dictator stood and addressed hundreds of thousands of Romans who approvingly thundered, "El Duce!" It was only eight short weeks ago that his lifeless body hung on display in Milan. A fitting end, I thought, as I looked down on the now empty piazza below.

Then there was the 1,028,500 square yards of beautifully planned grounds called, the Mussolini Forum, the dictator's own private recreation center. At that time the forum was being used as a U.S. Army rest center. It included a magnificent gymnasium, Olympic size swimming pool, theater, gardens and tennis courts. Everywhere I looked, I saw beautiful marble tiled walls, ceilings and floors, all overlooking the Tiber River.

It would take volumes to describe this wondrous city. There is the Basilica of St. Peter, started in 1506, and completed 180 years later. Michelangelo contributed to the beauty of this building. Underneath the altar of St. Peter's, the prince of the Apostles is buried. The basilica of St. John, the Lateran, is the most important Catholic temple in the world. The coliseum, built in 72 A.D., is the largest of the Roman amphitheaters. Gladiators fought here and Christians were fed to lions. I saw the monument to Victor Immanuel II, and the tomb of the unknown soldier, guarded twenty-four hours a day. The Pantheon, a temple dedicated to Pagan Gods in the 2nd century. If I had but one trip to make to Europe, I thought, it would be to the seven cities of Rome.

But that was before I saw Paris, with its beautiful women. The Arc de Triomphe, the Eiffel Tower, the Louvre, the Cathedral of Notre Dame, Napoleon's tomb, the Sacred Heart Basilica, the thirteen bridges crossing the Seine, the Place de Concord, where the Guillotine once stood. They say that Marie Antoinette's blood can still be found there. Paris is truly one of the most beautiful cities in the world.

⌘

With only one squadron at Istres, the base was more like a very small town and it wasn't long before you knew practically everyone in town. One unusual acquaintance I made was that of an occasional visitor to the base, a young interpreter for the MPs named Paul, from Avignon. His father was a judge in that fair city.

One day Paul said that his parent's would like to meet me, they had not talked to an American in years, he said. I accepted the invitation, and agreed to meet him the following Saturday at his father's house in Avignon. I boarded a bus in Istres and traveled north. All along the road were grim reminders of the war. As the German armies retreated north, American fighter planes were hot on their heels. Panzers and other vehicles, gutted by fire, were now rusting along the roadside.

Avignon is located on the banks where two rivers converge, the Rohne and Durance. As we approached, I could see that this was no ordinary place. Across the river the town is surrounded by walls. There are eight gates and thirty-nine towers. Rising above the town is a Cathedral, once the Papal Palace, situated on top of a hill. This city had been a byway on the road from Paris to Marseilles for centuries. But what really put it on the map and made it a tourist attraction for hundreds of years, is the fact that it was the capital of the Christian world in the 14th century. Seven French Popes once reigned here.

The bus crossed the river and entered one of the eight gates. We drove down tree lined streets to a large square brimming with sidewalk cafes and bustling boutiques. The bus stopped at the square, this was the end of the line.

There were no taxi cabs but I found a horse and carriage for hire. The driver could not speak English so I handed him the piece of paper Paul had written his father's address on. We clip-ity clop-ed down cobblestone streets in a residential area lined with high stucco walls. The carriage stopped at a curved arch spanned by wooden doors. The judge's address, posted on the wall next to the arch, told me I was there. I paid the driver and pulled the chain hanging from a bell mounted on the wall. A servant greeted me and led me through a beautifully landscaped courtyard to the entrance of the main house. I was ushered through a large marbled foyer to a magnificently furnished living room. As I stood on one of the most beautiful Persian rugs I have ever seen, Paul introduced me to his distinguished looking parents.

Paul was our interpreter. Although his parents could speak some English, they could not speak it fluently. I was served a very strong coffee in a demitasse cup and a liqueur glass of clear cognac. The judge said that it was 120 proof, and homemade.

His parents first asked me many questions about America and Detroit. Then they asked of my impressions of France. After telling of the good things I liked about their country, I mentioned something that troubled me about America's oldest Ally. Why, I asked, were the people in northern France so much more friendly than those in the south? People in the south seemed to resent my presence, I said, and I described a shocking incident in Istres when children asked me for chocolate. When I told them I had no chocolate they hissed, *"Boche good, Yank, no good!"* and spat at my feet.

Paul and his father talked for a few minutes, then Paul turned to me and said: "At first the Boche only occupied northern France and the coast. They signed an Armistice with Marshal Petain, creating Vichy, France, the unoccupied portion. Petain was a collaborator," he continued, "and even helped the Germans in rooting out French Jews. He opposed the Allies, especially De Gaulle. Consequently, Vichy, France was spared the horrors and deprivations experienced in the occupied north. That is, until November 1942, when Hitler broke the Armistice and occupied *all* of France. Petain will soon go on trial for his crimes, I might add," he said. [Marshal Petain was sentenced to death, but this sentence was commuted to life in prison, by, of all people, Charles De Gaulle! Petain died in prison in 1951.]

"When it came to the French resistance the Boche were ruthless," Paul said. "But, they were always well-disciplined soldiers. And if you obeyed his rules he did not bother you." Paul was interrupted by his father and then continued. "My father does not want you to misunderstand us. Most Frenchmen are eternally grateful to America and the American soldier. And we Frenchmen do not judge all Americans for the acts of a few, as we hope you do not judge all Frenchmen for the acts of men like Marshal Petain. But, when the Americans landed in southern France, there were some instances of looting and rape. Even today it is common to see drunken Americans supported by lamp poles, lying in gutters, or urinating in doorways, I am told."

I had heard stories of the looting and raping and I had been embarrassed more than once by my drunken countrymen. All I could do was apologize for their conduct.

Then Paul related another story that helped explain the animosity of some Frenchmen. He said that an American convoy carrying supplies to the troops in the north was once stopped by a roadblock. A band of armed Frenchmen came pouring out of the woods and relieved the surprised Americans of their goods. These men were members of a communist political organization not recognized by the Americans as a legitimate resistance group. The Americans called them bandits, but most Frenchmen in the area called them partisans.

A few weeks later another convoy was stopped in the same manner. But this time the French were surprised by Americans hidden in the trucks. The Americans opened fire and only a few Frenchmen escaped. Regardless of who was at fault, Paul said, the relatives and friends of these men considered them patriots. Good men, only trying to feed their families and fight the Boche.

⌘

It was almost dark out when I returned to the square to catch the bus back to Istres… only to find out that I had missed the last bus. So I decided to do what worked so well for me in England… and use my thumb. After the first hour, between walking and riding, I had covered perhaps ten miles and had a long way to go. It had been dark now for some time, of course there were no street lights in the barren countryside.

I had just passed my first rusting German panzer on the side of the road. It looked grotesque flooded by moonlight. I hadn't seen hide nor hair of a car in some miles now. I was beginning to get a little anxious. Finally, I heard the sound of an engine and saw two headlights coming up behind me. The headlights slowed and the brakes squealed as a GI truck pulled to a stop beside me. It was a Red Ball Express.

The Red Ball Express carried supplies to our servicemen just about everywhere. The door opened and a voice said, "Want a ride Sergeant?" I gladly hopped in, and thanked the driver, the first live black GI I had ever seen. We made some small talk. I told him I was stationed at the air base near Istres. He said he was going right through Istres. I mentioned how lucky I was that he came along.

When we got to Istres, without saying a word, he turned onto the road leading to the base and drove the two or three miles to the main gate so I wouldn't have to walk. He said "Good luck," I said "thanks," and got out.

Several days later, I asked a captain in the Military Police about Paul's story. He said that everything was true except the part about the partisans. "They were nothing but a bunch of God damned Commie Frogs, and got exactly what they deserved," he said… and so it goes.

Always hungry for news, we listened to the Armed Forces Radio and read the Stars and Stripes daily. We knew that, as the fighting in the Philippines was increasing in intensity, President Truman approved the invasion of Japan on June 29, 1945. And it was expected that more than one million lives would be lost in that invasion. Although I didn't know it at the time, my brother Wayne, was sitting on Okinawa with the 11th Airborne, waiting to jump into Japan, where casualties were expected to exceed eighty percent.

Our spirits brightened several days later when we learned that on August 6, the B-29 'Enola Gay' dropped a 'Super Bomb' destroying the Japanese city of Hiroshima. Then, just two days later, another Japanese city, Nagasaki, had been destroyed by another "Super Bomb." On that same day, the Soviet Union had at last declared war on Japan, and unleashed 1,500,000 troops on three fronts, completely smashing Japanese defenses in Asia. We were overjoyed, there was no doubt in our minds now that World War II would soon be over.

We then learned that the "Super Bomb" was an Atomic bomb, successfully tested at Alamagordo, New Mexico as recently as July 16. Not knowing if the bomb would work, Truman had continued to make plans for an invasion. It was after that test that he made the decision to use the bomb. That decision has been questioned by many since. But for the hundreds of thousands of American soldiers preparing to invade Japan, as well as their families back home, there *never* was a question regarding the President's decision.

There was a tragic sideline to the Enola Gay bombing, however. The U.S. Cruiser Indianapolis had delivered the bombs to the Air Force on Tinian, from which the Enola Gay would take off. From Tinian, the *Indy* went to Guam. From Guam she was to proceed to Leyte, where she would make preparations to participate in the invasion of Japan. However, on her way to Leyte she was sunk by a Japanese submarine, and over 900 crewmen perished. The irony of this disaster was, those 900 men had played such an important part in ending World War II, and they never lived to see it. But, as tragic as that was, imagine how the war might have changed had the *Indy* been sunk on the way *to* Tinian.

⌘

We were scheduled to fly a routine *Green Project* flight on August 12, that turned out to be anything but routine. Everything went well until we were about four hours out of Port Lyauty, on our way home. Instead of DPs on this trip, we carried some passengers from the 327th on their way to England.

Over the Mediterranean, just north of Barcelona, we ran into a terrible storm. Lightning virtually lit up the radio room. Hail, the size of marbles, battered the aircraft. Word from the cockpit said that the instruments were going crazy.

First JW tried to climb over the storm, but we no longer carried oxygen. He couldn't risk going much higher than ten thousand feet, and the storm was higher than that. Turning back was out of the question. We were beyond the point of no return.

Our only choice was to get around it, if that was possible. West to Spain was one option. East to more of the Mediterranean Sea was the other. JW elected to go west. If he had to set down, he preferred Spain to the turbulent sea. Of course, Spain was still a neutral country. As he turned west, he asked me to raise the base and report our position and present heading, but the storm prevented any radio contact with Istres. All I got was static.

Weather conditions improved as we neared the coast of Spain, then we turned north, following the coast. To the north were the Pyrenees Mountains. Istres, was Northeast.

Below, the beach was very wide, and JW considered landing, so he dropped down and buzzed it to take a look. It looked smooth enough, but everyone agreed, there was no way of telling if the sand was hard or soft. Attempting a landing on soft sand was just like committing suicide. The man up front wisely decided not to chance it.

Now we were coming up on the mountains dead ahead. France, and hopefully, safety, were just on the other side. Most of the peaks weren't all that high, so the man in the cockpit just snaked around the big ones and eventually flew out of them. Off to the east, the sky still looked bad, so when the guys up front spotted a small airfield, JW circled it. It had only one grass runway, but it looked long enough. A small building with a wind sock stood at one end next to what looked like a very small hanger. One single engine plane, similar to an L-5 'Recon,' was standing near the hanger. JW wanted to land here, so we all looked for possible holes in the ground as he buzzed the grass runway. It looked safe, so he turned and landed in the grass. He taxied up to the buildings and then cut the engines.

As we jumped out of the aircraft, two men in uniform approached us. They couldn't speak English but, fortunately, one of our passengers from the 327th could speak French. It turned out that these men were in De Gaulle's Free French Army, the army that had liberated this particular area. One of the men made a phone call from an old magneto telephone, then told us that transportation would soon be here to take us to a nearby village. While we waited JW suggested that I try and raise Istres again by running the trailing wire antenna out on the ground. I knew this wouldn't work, but he was the boss, so with Jaeger's help I tried anyway. I was right.

Before long two cars arrived. The first looked like it was right out of a Chicago gangster movie. It was a long black vintage limousine. A little man wearing a bow tie, dark suit with tails, and a top hat, stepped out of the limo. He introduced himself as the mayor of the village and said that he wanted to be the first to welcome us.

This was obviously wine country. On the ride into town we passed miles and miles of vineyards. Grapevines seemed to stretch as far as the hazy, blue-grey, Pyrenees, rising in the distance. At the village the limo stopped in front of a sidewalk café and bar on a typically narrow cobblestone street. The place was closed but the mayor soon changed that by banging on the door. Soon the proprietor was hovering over us with wine as others were busily preparing a meal. I'm sure that very scarce food supplies were somehow scrounged up in order to feed us.

After dinner, we moved to tables outside for more wine. Sitting there with the village VIPs we caused quit a sensation. The other side of the street was jammed with people trying to appear casual as they drifted back and forth to get a look at us. This village hadn't seen friendly foreigners in many years and had never seen live American airmen in flying suits.

Our money was no good, our hosts looked genuinely offended when we offered to pay. France could never repay you for what you have done for us, the mayor said. Later, we were shown to rooms in a small inn and we slept in a real bed that night. The next morning the mayor took us back to our plane and half the village followed.

Landing on this field had been risky enough for a heavy bomber but, taking off would be something else. The Free French had contacted Istres yesterday and relayed a message for us. We knew we had enough fuel, so now all we had to do was get this flying machine in the air. JW paced off the amount of runway he figured it would take to get us airborne, then we spread out at arms length and walked it, looking for holes. It was as smooth as a football field. When we caught up to JW he was squinting into the rising sun and scratching his head as he chewed on a long stem of grass. As we gathered around he took his hat from under his arm, cocked it on his head and said, "Let's get the hell out'a here!"

We bid farewell to our hosts, pulled the props through, and boarded the aircraft. JW taxied to a stand of pines, turned facing the grass-covered runway, revved up the engines and proceeded to make what seemed like the longest take off ever. He circled the field, roared over the waving crowd below and we were on our way home.

Three planes had left Port Lyautey on August 12. One had gone to the east to get out of the storm and had no problems. We had gone west. But the third had gone right through the storm. Our ground crew suggested we go and take a look at this aircraft. They said that we wouldn't believe it. And they were right. Most of the Plexiglas nose had been knocked out by hail as big as baseballs, it was said. The leading edge of the wings looked like someone had beat them with a ball-peen hammer. The crew chief said that all four engines and props would have to be changed. It was hard to believe that a plane could endure such a beating and still fly.

And then it finally happened. On August 15, 1945, we heard the official announcement on the radio and banner headlines in the Stars and Stripes announced:

"JAPAN QUITS"

The day was officially proclaimed VJ day. And again we were restricted to the base. Again our hearts were heavy as we listened to broadcasts of celebrations going on around the world. We longed to be home and envied those that were. I have never been as homesick as I was that day.

Fighting still went on though, as many stubborn Japanese refused to believe that the war was over. Those in Manchuria did not give up until August 22. In Malaya, it was September 12. And for some islands in the Pacific, it went on for weeks after that.

⌘

In the meantime, we had no idea when we were going home. Shortly after VJ day, all of my friends that had been sent back to the States for retraining had been discharged and were already home.

Letters from my father described a disturbing situation back home. Hundreds of thousands of servicemen were being discharged and were looking for work. Everyday thousands were consummating long delayed marriages creating a severe housing shortage.

⌘

One day, on a return flight from Port Lyautey, JW asked me if I wanted to fly the plane. I was delighted. Of course our copilot Bob, was at my side and all I really did was steer.

First, I had a problem steering 38,000 pounds of aircraft. When I saw that I was drifting to the left, I over corrected to the right, and then over corrected to the left. At the same time I saw that I was losing altitude and over corrected pulling up, and then over corrected going down. Consequently, I was zigzagging back and forth and going up and down. Finally Joe had had enough. How could he navigate like this, he asked. He suggested that I leave the flying to Bob.

The one and only time I flew a B-17

USFET
ATHLETIC OFFICE
presents

GI
WORLD
SERIES

Nurnberg SOLDIERS' FIELD
SEPT 8, 1945

On September 7, we, and another crew, pulled an assignment to transport some Armed Forces baseball teams from Reims, France, to Nuremberg, Germany. The Teams would participate in the GI World Series being played in Nuremberg. We were to stay, watch the series, and fly the teams back to Reims.

A shuttle drove us to our quarters near Soldiers' Field, in Nuremberg, where the games would be played.

As we passed through what was left of the city, our driver pointed out the building where twenty-one high-ranking Nazi, including Herman Goering, Rudolph Hess, Albert Speer, Joachim von Ribbentrop, Alfred Jodl, Wilhelm Keitel, and Karl Doenitz, were being held awaiting trial for war crimes. They would later be tried in the famous 'Nuremberg Trials.' [Before the trials were over, however, Herman Goering committed suicide.]

Most of the city was rubble. As far as I could see few buildings escaped some kind of damage. One whole wall was missing on a high-rise apartment building. It looked like a life size doll house. People were still living on every floor. They were going about their business in kitchens, living rooms, dining rooms, etc.

Hobnailed German soldiers, carrying back packs, were still walking home from whatever front they were on when the war ended. Most, no longer had a home to go to, and were just wandering.

When we checked into our quarters, we were warned to never go anywhere alone. In the previous week three American soldiers had been found murdered. They had been stripped naked. Even their dog tags were missing.

Between ball games I once walked the short distance to Luitpold Arena with a friend on the other crew. This mammoth arena was built for Hitler's Nazi party rallies which were held here annually from 1933 until the early 1940s. I had seen this place many times in newsreels. It was here that Hitler had ranted and raved to the world for so many years. I walked across the empty arena and climbed the marble stairs to the speaker's platform. The giant marble eagle whose large talons once grasped a huge Swastika, had been dynamited by the American 7th Army. Looking out over the arena, as in Rome, I could hear the ghosts of hundreds of thousands of German youth thunder "Sieg Heil! Heil Hitler!" And I thanked God that Hitler's "thousand" year Third Reich had ended long before his prediction, and I am proud that I had played a part in its ending.

23

THE GREEN PROJECT WAS TERMINATED ON SEPTEMBER 10, 1945.But we were still in that god forsaken place called Istres, and would be, for some time to come.

The Super Race in Istres, France, May 1945

⌘

It was in early September that I received a final letter from Annie. Reading between the lines I could only consider it a "Dear John" letter.

She suggested that we put our engagement on hold indefinitely. At least until she graduated and I finished my education in the States. Then we could take another look at it. I could see her father's fingerprints all over it. After all, he had plenty of time to brainwash her.

He knew that now I was just another Yank with a very uncertain future. He also knew that hundreds of thousands of veterans were flooding the colleges and job market back home, while I was stuck in France, and we had no idea how long I would be there.

At first I was heartbroken. But I had many friends in the 325th. . . we were family, and with their help I survived.

There are two lessons I learned here: "Absence *does not* make the heart grow fonder." And, "Time *does* heal all wounds."

September 18.
The Blue Project

With the Green Project over we were about to embark on an ill-fated hair-brained scheme that would first shake my faith in our State Department. I am sure that few people alive today ever heard of the *Blue Project.* This well intentioned but ill-conceived plan was designed to fly Greek DPs, whom the State Department called... slave laborers... stranded in Germany, back to their homeland.

Our crew was one of six chosen to kick off this grand scheme. We were to fly these DPs from Munich, Germany, to Athens, Greece. We flew to Munich on September 17th, and attended a briefing session that afternoon. Three crews would fly the first mission on the 18th. Three more would fly the second mission on the 19th. Fortunately, we were scheduled for the second mission and missed all the excitement.

The first three planes were loaded up and took off bright and early the next morning. Late that afternoon we were astonished when they returned with *all* passengers still aboard! After the planes were unloaded, the pilots reported an amazing story.

Someone had made a colossal miscalculation, they said. Once on the ground in Athens, *thousands* of angry Greeks surrounded the planes. Some were waving weapons and demanded to talk to the pilots. Through open windows the pilots were warned that *any* Greek leaving the plane would be shot on the spot. They were told that these, so-called *slave laborers,* were actually high paid skilled tradesmen and technicians who had been recruited by the Germans.

This did not mean that there were no slave laborers in Germany; in fact, there were many. What it did mean was that not all foreigners in German occupied countries were slave laborers. In any event, *The Blue Project* was canceled, and we were to return to Istres in the morning.

I have always found flying a most humbling experience. It makes one realize what a small place we take up on this great planet. And now, as Jaeger and I picked our way through the rubble of the once proud city of Munich, I also realized what a *fragile* world it is we live in.

Long ago, when Hitler was struggling for power in prewar Germany, he made a campaign promise: *"Give me four years,"* he said, *"and I promise you, you won't recognize your towns."* And that was one of the few campaign promises a politician ever kept.

Surrounded by the concrete, brick and steel of our large cities, I had always felt secure. We take it for granted that they will last for centuries. But in London, Nuremberg and Munich, I saw first hand how vulnerable they really are to modern warfare.

Pictures in magazines and newsreels are one thing, but actually walking through and around the rubble is another. We were forced to walk around the head of a giant stone eagle lying in the middle of the street. Many years ago a proud people had erected this marvel of carved stone high above their train station, believing that it would watch over their fair city for hundreds of years. Now it was nothing but tons of rock blocking the street.

Someone had told Jaeger about a 'blind pig' in the area and we were on our way to check the place out. I don't know why I let him twist my arm, for I was really apprehensive about straying too far from our quarters. Perhaps I didn't want him going alone. Whatever the reason, here I was picking my way through this rubble just for a few glasses of German beer. When I think back on it, it wasn't a very smart thing to do.

George laughed as we passed a store with no roof. "See that sign," he said, "it says, Now open twenty-four hours, every day." The sign was in German. I couldn't read it. But how did he know what the sign said?

Well, let me tell you. I had flown more than one thousand hours with this man, many of them combat hours, kicked a five-hundred pound bomb from a plane with him, and not once did I even suspect that he could speak German. I don't know why he never mentioned the fact. Evidently he wanted it that way. At least until the war was over.

Although many Germans could speak passable English, Jaeger's ability to speak their language made our evening in the bar that night much more meaningful. About half the patrons in the bar were very elderly German men. The other half were guys like us, American soldiers. Only, I noticed *they* were armed.

We found a strange thing about post war Germany… *there were no Nazi left!* And you couldn't find anyone that ever *had* been a member of the Nazi party. And the men in this bar were no exception. However, they were not without opinions concerning Americans and how the Allies won the war. I found that their opinions did not differ very much from their PW sons back at Istres.

Their idea of Americans and America, was a classic example of what propaganda can do. Doctor Goebbels had done his job well. Every German I talked to *sincerely* believed that the great majority of Americans lived like the Joad's in *The Grapes of Wrath*. And that a handful of rich and powerful Jews controlled the country, keeping the masses in utter poverty and there was no convincing them otherwise.

They believed that we won the war because we overwhelmed them with numbers. Men, tanks, planes, guns, jeeps... everything... and there is no doubt, some truth to that.

Besides, they could never figure out what the Americans were going to do next, they said. How could they? The Americans were so confused even *they* didn't know what they were going to do next. How can you fight a war like that? They asked. And there probably was some truth to that.

When asked why they fought on when all was obviously lost, they usually gave several reasons. One was, they were convinced that the Allies were intent on annihilating the German race. The fire bombings of Berlin and Dresden had convinced them of that. Another was, Goebbels had promised them that a new 'Super' weapon was about to be unleashed and that the tide would soon turn in their favor. No doubt Goebbels had in mind the Atomic bomb.

I had to drag George out of that bar. He was so intent on conversation, he hadn't noticed that we were the last Americans in there and it was dark outside. Things looked a lot different outside in the moonlight. The eerie skeletons of the bombed-out buildings were grotesque.

Remembering the story of the dead GI's found in Nuremberg, I expected Germans to pop out from every building and I wondered why I had ever let my friend talk me into this excursion. Eventually we found the friendly lights of the guard house, though, and were soon safely in bed.

⌘

Then one day we flew to Lyon. I don't remember why, but I know we RONd. Approaching Lyon from the air is a spectacular sight. With the Alps in the background you see this huge hill of a city between the Saone and Rhone Rivers just before they converge. I was really impressed with Lyon. It is a very interesting and old city. At one time it was the capital of Gaul. When I was there, there was an original road still in use built by the Romans centuries ago.

If you have an interest in history, fine food and good wine, especially Beaujolais, you must visit this wonderful city and the Beaujolais vineyards nearby. Some of the best cooking schools and restaurants in the world are in Lyon. I liked this city so much I came back and spent a seven-day leave there with Clair, a very pretty French nurse who volunteered to be my guide.

⌘

Things were winding down fast now at Istres. On September 25, we pulled an assignment to fly men from our squadron to Little Walden, England. They were on the first leg of their journey home. We RONd at Little Walden due to bad weather. In the morning we flew to Bury St. Edmonds to refuel. Then, just after taking off from Bury, we smelled smoke, and JW said that our number *one, two,* and *four* engines were in trouble.

The tower at Bury instructed him to proceed to Alconbury, near Peterburough for maintenance.

Alconbury was the only base left in the United Kingdom equipped to provide maintenance on B-17s. For a while it was nip and tuck whether we were going to make it or not. We did, and were stranded for three days in Alconbury while repairs were being made.

While there, I learned that I was a short bus ride from Glatten, where brother Glen spent his time in England. So I went to Glatten just to tell brother Glen that I had been there.

Back at Istres the population gradually dwindled. A slow evacuation was underway. In the meantime we all shared one emotion... a terrible longing to be home. The days and nights seemed to get longer with each passing day. To while away time I spent many afternoons swimming in a large salt water lake called Etang de Berre. Many evenings were spent drinking beer in the PX and on rare occasions watching one of the many 'crap' games that seemed to pop up almost everywhere.

At long last I received orders to leave, and with mixed emotions I bid farewell to my friends and boarded a B-17 as a passenger. Strangely, I felt bewildered and very lonely. I knew I would never see my comrades again. And I also knew that this would be my last flight on the aircraft that I had become so attached to. The flight terminated at Roughem, England, near Bury St. Edmonds. I had been transferred to the 94th Bomb

Group, the 332nd Squadron, scheduled to leave for the USA soon.

On December 8, 1945, at the port of Southampton, we boarded the Queen Mary, the historic ship that is now docked in Long Beach, California. The next day, at 1:00 P.M. at long last, I was now on *my* sentimental journey home.

It was a real emotional experience. I had longed for this moment for so long... and yet... as I watched the shores of England slip away, there was a lump in my throat. So much had happened in this last year. I felt guilty leaving behind so many comrades that would never make this trip. Even to this day I can visualize so many faces. Faces of young men who will never grow old. Tom Shanahan writing letters home looks the same to me today as he did in the day room in 1945.

My heart ached as I saw Annie, smiling up at me as we danced. It was hard to imagine never seeing her again.

When I could see land no more, I turned and went below decks, knowing that there was no place like the U.S.A., but there would always be a bond between me and the great country of Britannia. Even though I knew it would never be the same, I vowed to someday come back.

⌘

So there I was, on the worlds most famous luxury liner at one time, now converted into a troop ship. All I can say is that it was a horrible trip. We encountered a terrible storm. Scuttlebutt had it that two LSTs carrying troops broke up in those storms.

Even though I believe the ship must be more than four stories high, we got soaking wet one day by waves crashing over the bow.

We held our trays down at mess so they wouldn't slide away. Some men were so sick they threw up at the dinner table, which made things much more difficult for the rest of us.

⌘

Then on December 13, 1945, we saw one of the most beautiful sights in the world, the Statue of Liberty. We anchored near New Jersey and spent the rest of the day disembarking onto ferries that carried us to shore. The only people here to greet us were Red Cross girls passing out small cartons of milk, God bless them for being there, I wanted to kiss them all. There were no ticker tape parades, but I understood that. After all, the war in Europe had ended almost seven months ago.

⌘

We were trucked to waiting trains which shuffled us to Camp Atterbury Indiana. After what seemed to be endless days of what the Army called processing, I was issued my discharge on December 19, 1945. Several days later I disembarked from a train at the Fort Street

Station in Detroit and was greeted by my family, except for my brother Wayne. He was now a member of the occupation forces in Japan.

Separation Center, Camp Atterbury, Indiana, Debermber 19, 1945

I had left home on September 11, 1943 and returned on December 21, 1945. The best Christmas present I ever had

Epilogue

Saturday, April 17, 1965

I climbed the white marble stairs to the entrance of the Veterans Memorial Building on Jefferson Avenue, in Detroit, Michigan. I was on my way to a U.S. Savings Bond Drive luncheon being held there. As I entered the huge marble hall, I noticed the bronze plaques on the walls honoring the servicemen from Detroit who had given the ultimate gift to their country in World War II.

My hair tingled and goose bumps traveled down my arms and back, as I realized that it was exactly twenty years ago *today* that my friend had gone down over Dresden.

I find it hard to express my feelings as I stood in that great hall scanning the names beginning with 'S,' hoping not to find Tom's. All these years my conscious mind had refused to believe that Tom was dead. I wanted to believe that he would some day show up. But there it was, I could deny it no longer. Carved in Bronze, it read:

SHANAHAN, THOMAS, J.

Tears came to my eyes and I unsuccessfully tried to choke back a sob. Somehow I felt as though Tom was up there on that wall looking down at me. I could see him in the day room, smoke rising from his pipe as he wrote letters home.

I recently visited the war memorial to the men who died in Vietnam. The phenomenon I saw at the wall helps me to understand my feelings on that day in 1965. Hundreds and hundreds of people were viewing the wall... a wall of names, names of former comrades, friends or relatives. And everyone... *everyone,* had tears in their eyes. And some were, unsuccessfully, trying to hold back a sob.

In January 1946, I called his home. His mother choked up, sobbing. His father took the phone and apologized, suggesting that I wait awhile before calling back. I gave him my number, in case they wanted to talk. I was confused; I know Tom told them about me, and thought they would appreciate my carrying out his request. The experience shook me up so much, I never called back. I thought that it was up to them to call me. I never did hear from them.

Over fifty-thousand B17 crewmen were killed in the 8th Air Force during the war. Tom Shanahan wasn't my only friend to die during those terrible times. Many were the days I would have breakfast with comrades, only to count their empty bunks that evening. Oh those empty bunks! God, how can I ever forget their faces. . . and their empty bunks!

John Paul, Tom Shanahan's pilot, 1994

Thanks to the 92nd Bomb Group Memorial Corporation, in 1994 I located John Paul, Tom Shanahan's pilot. In a telephone conversation with John that year I learned that I had mistakenly thought that I had talked to John after the big collision on April 17. As it turned out, it was another officer that I had talked to, not John, as reported in my earlier versions.

John Paul told me that I *had* probably talked to his tail gunner. It was true that they were the only survivors. He had been able to bail out and was captured by the Germans. After spending some time incarcerated in what he called 'Camp Lucky Strike,' he was liberated by the British, and was sent directly to Southampton, where he was transported by ship to the States. He never went back to Podington, he said.

As for Tom, he said that Tom's body was found after the war. He is now buried in Arlington Cemetery. John said that he visited Tom's parents in Detroit after the war. I still can't figure out why they saw him, but never returned my call.

When John Paul learned that I was living near Tony Marozas, in Lisle, Illinois, at that time, he asked if I would do him a favor and pay his old copilot a visit.

Tony Marozas, Tom Shanahan's copilot, 1994

In the summer of 1994 I met with Tony Marozas in Lisle, and recorded a lengthy conversation with him. Tony said that he flew fourteen missions with John and Tom, then obtained his own crew as pilot.

He was shot down over Fassberg on April 4, 1944. He was able to keep the aircraft airborne long enough for his crew to bail out. Then he bailed out at 3,000 feet. German soldiers were waiting for them as they landed, he said. Everyone surrendered except his navigator, who ran, and was immediately shot in the knee by a German soldier with a burp gun. They were later liberated and returned to Podington.

His navigator's leg was in a cast but became infected and later had to be amputated. Tony thought it could have been his navigator's cast that I had signed back in Podington. I still have the tape of our conversation.

Sadly, not long after my interview, Tony Marozas joined his compatriots somewhere up there... far above 32,000 feet.

Harry Culver, 1994

I also learned through the 92nd Memorial Corporation that Harry Culver and his crew had survived. The last time I saw his aircraft it was going down into the heart of Berlin. In a telephone conversation with Harry in 1994, I learned that he was able to get the aircraft to Sweden and landed at Malmo, where the crew was interned until the war ended.

Hank Lapinski, 1995

It had been fifty years since I had last seen Hank Lapinski. And fifty-two years since Hank had introduced me to his lovely wife Betty at a restaurant in Ardmore, Oklahoma. Hank had taken the whole crew out to dinner to meet Betty. Thanks again to the 92nd Memorial Corporation, we were reunited in April 1995. Hank and Betty spent two days golfing and reminiscing with my wife Martha and I at our home in Florida. We have been meeting in Florida almost every year since 1995. We also communicate by mail and telephone

George Waldschmidt

The only other crew-member I have seen since the war was also at that dinner in Ardmore in 1944. I visited George Waldscmidt and his lovely wife Joella at their home in Fort Wayne, Indiana sometime in the late fifties. We sat in his living room for several hours. Among other things we discussed the Berlin mission of February 3rd and the Dresden mission of February 14.

Imagine my surprise, while browsing through the June 1990 issue of the 92nd Bombardment Group NEWS publication, when I read a story about George written by a John Schroeder. Briefly, it tells of how George, a talented art student before the war, happened to paint a ten-foot mural of a B-17 on the wall of the 325th Squadron Ready Room at the request of Colonel Wilson. Also, included in that issue are pictures of that mural in the process of being restored.

Now imagine how devastated I was when I next picked up the issue of September 1991, and read the front page story by Mr. David Lee, Director of the Duxford Museum, in which he reported that George Waldschmidt had died in December of 1989.

Sadly, George died shortly before he was to be honored when his mural, he called, "The Big Picture," went on display at the Duxford Imperial War Museum. The *whole* section of the wall on which the mural was painted had been moved from Podington to Duxford, where it was restored, and is now on display.

I vividly remember spending hours watching George, on his ladder, paint that mural in the ready room. Many gallons of paint were spread over a canvas on the floor. I had always thought of myself as a frustrated artist, but as I watched, I knew that I was no match for this man.

I have many fond memories of George. He spent many hours talking to me in the radio room during boring practice flights. His back against the wall, arms hugging his knees. George had a very probing mind. I remember the time he popped his chest pack chute all over the radio room floor. He said, he always wondered if it would really work. Then there were the times he wanted to pull the pin on the IFF... to see if it would really blow up.

It was George who talked me into riding in the ball turret on a practice flight one evening. And it was then that I discovered what courage this man had. How anyone could spend so many hours in a fetal position, surrounded

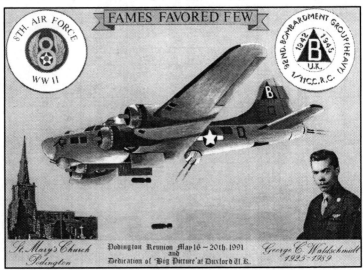

George Waldschmidt's "The Big Picture," The Imperial War Museum, Duxford, England, 2001

by a Plexiglas ball suspended *below* the aircraft, is beyond me.

He got in that ball shortly after we took off for a mission and normally, could not get out until we were about to enter the landing pattern at Podington. In that time he constantly scanned the skies for Bandits. He had the most magnificent view of anyone on the crew. He saw more of everything going on out there than anyone else and he saw it better. The fighters, the flak, aircraft blowing up or going down in flames, his comrades bailing out, he saw it all. I thank God that there were men like George Waldschmidt. We owe them so much.

I had talked to George's wife in 1999 by phone. But Hank sadly told me in his visit in 2001, that she had recently passed away.

Danny Darnell was eighteen years old in 1945 when I was based at Podington. He worked for the Red Cross, relative to the enlisted mens Aeroclub. A club where enlisted men could gather and relax. Danny lived [and still does] just a few miles from Podington in the village of Bozeat.

After the war Danny became a commercial artist and an expert on paint, and restoration. In 1989 he was hired to supervise the restoration of George Waldschmidt's "The Big Picture" which is now in The Imperial War Museum at Duxford. Danny expected to meet George at the ceremony celebrating the completion of the restoration. Unfortunately, George died before the ceremony.

He then started to write a book about Podington, and George's picture. Looking for someone who flew with George, and knew him, he wrote me in January of 1998. Danny's letter kindled a friendship that lasts to this day.

In June 2001, my wife Martha and I met with Danny and his friend, Mark Jordan, of Wellingborough, at Duxford, England, to view George's restored picture. It was the first time I had been to the U.K. since 1945.

* You can find more information about the 92nd Bomb Group and Georges "Big Picture" on the Internet Web Site, **92NDMA.ORG.** Once on the web site, click on 92nd Bomb Group, then the "Big Picture." You will see Hank Lapinski and other dignitaries standing by Georges picture.

Al Vermeire, 1996

In 1996 I located and talked to my Squadron Lead Pilot Al Vermeire by phone. We have talked several times since. These telephone conversations have enabled me to present a much more accurate version of several missions. Al sent me a copy of the 92nd Bomb Group's 'Crew of the Week' award, the Army's official version of our part in the Bremen raid on March 11, 1945. He also confirmed the Molbis bomb kicking mission.

92nd Bomb Group Reunion, Savannah, Georgia, September, 2002.

It was my first reunion. Hank Lapinski was there with his wife Betty, and Al Vermeire was there with his wife. I had talked to Al on the phone, but this was the first time I had seen him since 1945. J. Bob Johnson, Al's radio operator whom I replaced when he was transferred to Ringsred's crew, was there with his wife. I met others for the first time, like Archivist Bob Elliot and Secretary Treasurer Irving Baum.

We had a wonderful time touring Savannah and the 8th Air Force museum. What I enjoyed the most was our sessions in the hospitality room. It's not surprising that you can learn much more about a man after he's had a few cocktails. I learned some things that I had never known before about my good friend Hank Lapinski, as well as many others.

You may recall that soon after I replaced J. Bob Johnson, Ringsred had to abort and land at Malmo, Sweden, where the crew was interned until the war was over. While in the hospitality room we heard some of his stories of life in Sweden, waiting for the war to end. I found the hospitality room to be a wealth of information that I could not have obtained in any other way.

The Queen Mary, 1990

Back in 1990, my son James [by my first marriage] had a Chiropractic practice in LA, not far from Long Beach, where the Queen Mary is docked. When we visited him that year I took a sentimental trip through the old liner with Jim, and my present wife Martha. It certainly brought back some memories, both good, and bad.

Annie

Although I changed her name and where she lived, this is a reasonably accurate account of the part my first love played in my life. Oversimplified and condensed... but reasonably accurate. Annie helped me get through some of the most difficult times of my life. I will never forget her, I owe her so much. There will always be a place in my heart for her.

Brother Wayne

As for Brother Wayne, thanks to the Atomic bomb, he did not have to parachute into Japan. Instead, he became part of the occupation forces in Japan and was discharged in December 1946. Sadly, brother Wayne passed away in 1999.

Brother Glen

Glen resides at his home in Royal Oak, Michigan.

Movies about B17s in World War II

12 O'clock High... in my opinion, not perfect, but the best from Hollywood.

The documentary... Memphis Bell (the real thing).

The Hollywood version of Memphis Bell, hammed up and very poorly done.

The War Lover... not bad, some very good combat scenes.

Command Decision... good movie.

Breinigsville, PA USA
17 January 2010
230882BV00005B/67/A